Coaching the Dream

A Parent's Guide: "No one cares about your child more than YOU!

Deborah H. Johnson

Dedication

This book is dedicated to my dream team. I thank the Lord for trusting me with the responsibility to advocate for sports parents and for providing me with everything that I need to get the job done. So much of who I am comes from my mom, Geneva Hubbard. She taught me the value of being a "hands on" advocate and having unconditional love for my children. I so wish she could be here to see this book in print. I am so thankful for my husband, Glen, who unselfishly and lovingly supports me and my dreams. My amazing sons, Jay, Joshua Alexander and Joshua Odis, have been the training ground for me to earn my certification as a sports parent advocate. They are the best sons I could have ever asked for and I am so proud of them. Thank you all! I love you!

Table of Contents

Acknowledgements

I am so thankful for the love and support that I have received from my family. From the beginning, they have believed in me and supported me in so many crucial ways. Thank you, my sisters Lois Branch and Sylvia Johnson for reading every chapter and provided me with so much feedback. Thank you Darrel and Rocki Branch for spending countless hours helping me to develop every aspect of my sports parent advocacy business and reading the manuscript. Thank you, Ed Hubbard, my brother and accomplished author who, long ago, shared with me your formula for writing and for being available to do mini-workshops just to teach me something I need to know. Thank you Wannie (my niece, Lawan Williams), an amazing writer and editor who took time out of two of your vacations to ensure this book was setup properly. Thank you my sisters Leona Hubbard Butler, Janice Bush and Sue Simpson, you never tire of listening to my plans and dreams even at all hours of the night. Thank you my brothers Harold Goldsmith and Jermaine Hubbard, you are a constant encouragement and great sources of wisdom. I am so blessed to have a huge family who inspire me and are the wind beneath my wings.

I am indebted to a host of other friends and professionals who have helped me in so many ways. Thank you, Reuel Barksdale, Sharon Lopez, Julia Marshall, Sheryl

Owens, Chandler Sirmons and Valerie Tutson for your unwavering encouragement and all of your help over the years. Thank you, Leah and Keith Wheeler for all your love and support and help with content. Thank you Mia Jackson, my co-host at Game Ready Mom Radio for sharing so many stories and helping me to see the details. Thank you Lorraine Clark for being obedient and helping me to see that I was a sports parent advocate. Thank you Coach Tressel, for supporting my involvement with the Ohio State University Football Program. Also, I am grateful for the amazing staff at Ohio State Sports Medicine whose expertise I rely on for so many things. And, thank you to all the parents of the Football Parents Association at Ohio State.

Lastly, thank you to the many unnamed parents and friends who shared their stories and who trust me to get involved with their child's sports career.

To God be the glory!

Introduction
Before the Dream

The Roots of a Dream

I love sports. I always have. Even as a little girl with five sisters, flat feet and less-than-perfect coordination, I had a deep and undying love for sports.

Sadly, those qualities meant I was never a stand-out athlete, but that didn't stop me from playing kickball and softball with my friends. By the time I was in high school, I was one of the loudest members of the booster club, yelling cheers at the top of my lungs to support our school's teams. But without a doubt, my favorite sport was football. I had lots of friends on the football team, and I loved to watch their games.

After high school, I enrolled at The Ohio State University—where football is a way of life—and my love of the game only increased! During those years, Woody Hayes was coaching, and people came from all over the world to watch the Buckeyes play. I got season tickets all four years, and I didn't miss a home game while I was a student.

Even now, nothing much has changed. I am still a sports fanatic. I love to watch almost every sport, and I enjoy all levels of competition, from pee wee leagues to the Olympics. In my mind, sports provide opportunities to challenge ourselves and achieve great things, opportunities that we cannot find in any other arena of life. Most importantly, the lessons we learn in the world of athletics are some of the most easily applied to our everyday lives, making us not just good athletes, but better human beings.

That is why I always hoped, one day, that my children would love sports as much as I do.

For a long time, that idea was just that...a hope. It was not a dream. It was a seed, a quiet and unspoken desire for something that might never actually happen.

Then I became a mom.

As one of five girls, I just assumed that I would also have girls. I was so sure my firstborn would be a girl; I even got some of my baby clothes from my mom for her.

But that is not how life turned out. Although I am certain that having daughters would have been wonderful and that they would have loved sports like I do, my first child was a boy, as was my second and my third!

And since the day that my oldest, Jay, was born, I have been amazed to discover how God has used my love of sports to nurture the sons He gave me.

Seeds of a Dream

From the start, Jay was destined to be an athlete. As a baby, his favorite toy was a multicolored cloth ball with bells inside. He was born long for his age, always taller and bigger than most of his peers, and he could run. While we lived on Guam, he earned the title of "Fastest 4-Year Old" and won a talking teddy bear in the Annual Teddy Bear Run.

As a preschooler, it was clear that Jay had athletic talent, and even that early, my dream for him began to take shape. I wanted him to be an athlete. I wanted him to excel in sports. I wanted to watch him compete and encourage him, through sports, to grow into the man that he was created to become. That was my dream.

And perhaps, that is your dream as well. If you are reading this book, you probably have a similar plan for your children. You, too, long to encourage a love of sports in your child. You appreciate the benefit of persevering and practice, of learning to win and to lose, and you want your child to learn those life skills, too. And perhaps, you are even hoping that an athletic path will lead your child to great success: first-place trophies, championship games, college scholarships and more.

If that is where you are, then I have to tell you—I understand. Like you, I am a sports parent. I have walked those paths and lived those lessons with my sons. I know where you are coming from, and I have been where you are (or soon will be). And I want you to know that I wrote this book for you.

I have a dream for you, too. I'm sure that sounds strange since I don't know you, but it's true. I have a heart and passion for sports parents. I want to encourage you. I hope to arm you with information and ideas that will help you navigate the sometimes-crazy world of athletics. I pray that God would see fit to use me to help you nurture your children, so that they can not only achieve their athletic dreams, but also use those dreams to discover and live out their God-given purpose in life. Simply put, my dream for you is that you will be equipped to be the best sports parent that you can be.

And to do that, I need to tell you more of our story.

Chapter One

It All Starts with a Dream

"Nothing happens unless first a dream." Carl Sandburg

Finding a Dream

Unfortunately, having a dream for my sons wasn't enough. They had to develop their own dream. And in seventh grade, Jay, did exactly that.

We had returned from Guam to live in Columbus, Ohio, where I happily watched the Buckeyes play every chance I got. Jay, on the other hand, found a different interest. During fourth grade, he began playing youth league soccer. I loved to watch him play, and he soon began to excel. During his first season, he even scored a goal from midfield! When a fellow spectator told me that few professional players could do that, I started to realize that Jay truly did have the potential to be an exceptional athlete.

Still, in our school district, students had to wait until seventh grade to play school sports. By that time, Jay's athletic build was even more obvious, and I desperately hoped to see him play football. I was also going through a divorce and wondering how I would pay for college. My inner voice kept whispering that Jay's athletic and academic ability would be all he needed to get through college, but Jay still wasn't sold on the idea.

In fact, Jay was far more interested in shooting hoops with his friends than playing football. Still, I didn't give up. Several times over the summer, I asked him about going out for the football team. Each time he told me he would think about it, but didn't think he wanted to play. I was disappointed but tried not to let it show. I just kept encouraging him to think about it.

All of that changed on the first day of school. At lunchtime, he called me at work, bubbling over with excitement. His math teacher, who happened to be engaged to the football coach, took one look at him and told him he looked like a football player and should try out for the team. With her encouragement, he decided to go for it. So he called me to ask if I could bring him some cleats so that he could try out that afternoon. I was so excited I could hardly contain myself. I left work, went to the store and bought his first pair of football cleats.

Needless to say, he made the team.

Living the Dream

That day was the beginning of Jay's dream to play football. It is a passion that continued through middle school, high school, college and even into the NFL. But just having the dream is not enough. A dream has to be lived out to be achieved. Jay began to practice and to play; he learned to love the game, to be part of a team, to push himself to be the best he could be. And I loved sharing every minute of it with him.

Of course, things weren't always easy for him. Right before Jay started tenth grade, I remarried, and we moved four blocks away—into a different school district. This was a difficult transition for Jay. He had played for four years in his previous school district, and now he had to start all over.

To make sure that Jay got a good start at the new school, I took him to register and to inquire about football conditioning. Before I could even ask, the woman helping us in the guidance office blurted out, "Has Jay met Coach Snyder?" When I told her that he hadn't, she jumped up from her desk and went out to get him. Jay began to condition with the team that day, and by the fall, he was a starting at defensive tackle.

The following year, the school hired a new coach, and Jay was moved to defensive end. A change like that can be very frustrating for a young athlete, but thankfully, Jay excelled at his new position. It was obvious that all the hard work Jay had done since middle school was paying off, and after his junior year, Jay began to get letters from colleges all over the country. We were both thrilled. I was actually watching my dream for him coming true. And by this time, Jay had a dream for himself—to play football for The Ohio State University—a dream I was happy to dream along with him!

The next two years were full of major events. In March of Jay's junior year, his coach called me at work. He asked if I was sitting down. After assuring me that nothing was wrong, he shared the good news: Jay has gotten his first scholarship offer. I sat at my desk and just wept.

Soon, offers from Division I schools began to pour in. We attended Junior Days at different universities so Jay could see the schools and meet the coaches. He enjoyed each visit, but still insisted that Ohio State was his school of choice. I, too, wanted him to go to Ohio State. It was my alma mater, and when you live in central Ohio, playing for OSU is tantamount to being in the NFL. But I also knew his dream would not be easy to reach. Jay was good, but was he *that* good? Ohio State had only about 25 spots in their recruiting class, and players from all over the country also wanted to make that roster. Still Jay kept working hard, and we remained hopeful that his dream offer would come.

While we waited, we kept visiting other schools. In April 2001, I took Jay to Michigan State University (MSU) and University of Michigan (U of M) for recruiting visits. Given the rivalry between Ohio State and Michigan, Jay wasn't keen on U of M. But it is a well-respected school which provides a top-notch education, and I thought Jay should check it out and make that decision for himself.

We started at MSU, intending to visit U of M afterward. The mini-camp lasted longer than I expected, but Jay got the award for best defensive player, and the recruiting coach invited us to attend their practice. We went, but I kept an eye on the clock because I wanted Jay to see U of M before it got dark. Just when I had decided we needed to get on the road, we were told that the head coach wanted to meet us. It was almost 6:30 pm, and our goal of covering both campuses was quickly fading. (We eventually got to U of M, but not until the late evening. Thankfully Jay was later invited to their 2001 Elite Camp, so he did get a proper introduction to the U of M program!)

We sat down with Coach Williams who wasted no more of our time. He told Jay that he liked him, and regardless of who else was recruiting Jay, they were offering him a full scholarship. I was stunned! I still had not grasped just how talented Jay was, and I was humbled that God had not only answered my prayer for a scholarship, but He gave Jay a choice of schools he could attend! Jay thanked him, looked him in the eye—and turned him down. He told Coach Williams that he really appreciated the offer, but right then, his first choice and his dream was to attend The Ohio State University, even though he had not been offered a scholarship yet.

I listened to my son's response with a bit of anxiety. I, too, was hoping for an offer from Ohio State, but what if that offer never came? Jay, on the other hand, never wavered, and my husband was confident, too. But still, there was no guarantee. I continued to pray and talk to Jay about what he would do if his dream offer didn't come.

Then, on July 1, 2002, Jay attended Ohio State's senior camp. Halfway through the morning, he called me. The coach wanted me to come to a luncheon for players and parents. So, of course, I went. It was pouring rain outside, and thoughts about Jay's future were pouring into my head as I drove to campus. Every week, the newspaper reported the players to whom Ohio State had offered scholarships. Now on one of the dreariest days of summer, I sloshed through the rain, wondering if Jay's offer would be in the next report.

As I parked outside the Woody Hayes Athletic Facility, the rain became torrential, and I had to run to keep from getting soaked. Coach Conley, the recruiting coach, was holding the door for me. As I stepped inside, he asked me if Jay had told me the news. I said no—Jay had only invited me for lunch. He asked again, "Did Jay tell you *the news*?" My heart began to pound with excitement, but I again said no. Chuckling, he told me they had asked Jay not to tell anyone, but they hadn't meant me, too. And I suddenly realized what he was saying—Jay's dream had come true!

He had gotten his offer to play football for The Ohio State University.

I felt like the sun had come out! I was simply overjoyed, and as a woman who is never at a loss for words, I suddenly found myself speechless. We were right in front of all the players and parents, so Coach Conley graciously took me down the hall so that I could jump up and down and celebrate—and that is exactly what I did!

That day was the fulfillment of many years of dreaming. Jay played for four years for the college of his dreams, and the team won the 2002 National Championship during his freshman year. The journey was an amazing one. It took years of hard work and prayer, but it all started with a dream.

It all Starts with a Dream

Dreams are part of life. They are real and important. They make us who we are. And they are different for everyone.

But one this is certain: every child has a dream, including yours. Some of those dreams will include sports; others will not. However, while much of this book can be applied by any parent to any dream, my heart is most passionate about helping sports parents successfully steer their students through the amazing and sometimes exhausting world of student athletics.

From experience, I can tell you that the world of student athletics is both exhilarating and complicated. The path will be winding and difficult. It is filled with ups and downs. But it can be navigated successfully, and I want to share with you, a sports parent like myself, what you can do to help your student achieve his or her dreams.

So where do you, as a parent, begin?

The Source of all Dreams

Generally, I find it best to start at the beginning—in this case, the beginning of a dream. If we think about it, we will probably all agree that dreams don't just pop into being out of nothing. Like everything else in existence, they have to come from somewhere. But where does a dream begin?

Some say that dreams begin in our hearts or our minds. Others see them rise out of our past, our present circumstances or our hopes for the future. However, I see dreams as bigger than any of those things; I believe that dreams are about more than merely our own selves.

I am convinced that all dreams, including a child's dream to play a sport, come from one Source. I believe all dreams are gifts from God. I believe this as surely as I believe that your child's love of sports can lead her to amazing places, just like Jay's did for him. And this belief forms the ideas that I am going to share with you throughout this book. To put it simply, I believe in God. I believe He speaks to us through the Bible. And I believe, absolutely, that our dreams come from Him.

But why would God give us dreams? So that He can use us.

I believe that dreams are directly tied to our purpose, that God uses our dreams as the fuel, the motivation, that enables us to become the men and women that He wants us to be. Proverbs 29:18 says, "Where there is no vision, the people perish." In other words, without dreams, people are lost. They wander through life without a sense of where they're going and why. But with dreams, with a clear sense of purpose, people prosper—they move forward and grow. It's exactly what Carl Sandburg's meant when he said:

"Nothing happens unless first a dream." Our dreams are the catalyst to get us where we need to go.

This has been true in my own life. My love for sports gave rise to a dream that my sons would play football (or any other sport they loved). But I had no idea that my passion for athletics would open doors for me to become an advocate for sports parents, a public speaker for parents and students, and (now) an author! I am convinced that God gave me my passion for sports so that He could use it to make me what He wanted me to be, so that He could use me to encourage you.

God has done the same for Jay. I know God gave Jay a dream to play football so that, through that dream, He could abundantly bless and provide for Jay. All through Jay's life, God was regularly at work, directing Jay's path and providing incredible opportunities, open doors that I could never have imagined or created on my own.

For example, when I remarried and Jay was moved to a new school district in tenth grade, it seemed like a huge problem. But that change of address was, instead, a blessing in disguise. His former school had almost one hundred players on the team, many of them experienced upperclassmen. As a sophomore, Jay wasn't likely to start on that team. But at the new school, he gained lots of experience as well as a starting position.

Jay's dream also provided him the chance to get a world-class education. When I first began nurturing Jay's talent for sports, I couldn't know that I would eventually be divorced, remarried and wondering how we would afford his college tuition. But all of that did happen, and I did not know where the money would come from. Thankfully, God knew, and He provided a full scholarship for Jay.

Looking back, it is so clear to me that God used Jay's talent to open doors for my son. Sports provided Jay a ready-made support group of teammates and friends. When he changed school in the middle of high school, it was football that helped him cope. In a matter of weeks, Jay got to know the other football players, and when school actually started, he had met teachers and knew his way around the new campus. Football made for an almost seamless transition from one district to the other.

Football also provided amazing connections, opportunities that God has used to shape Jay into the man He wanted Jay to become. At the U of M Elite Camp in 2001, Jay met Bo Schembechler. At the time, he had no idea the living legend that Bo was, but I knew, and I was so excited. I took their picture, and when Bo hugged Jay, he told him "Young Man, don't you know the folks in Columbus would have a fit if they saw you hugging me!" Sadly, in November 2006, on the day before Jay's final game in the Shoe (against Michigan!), Bo Schembechler died. But thankfully, by then, Jay had developed a real appreciation for Bo and his legacy. (And that game was arguably the biggest game in the Shoe in OSU football history.)

Perhaps most significantly, God opened the door for Jay to play for Coach Jim Tressel, a Christian man and mentor. When Jay came to Ohio State, Coach Tressel had just taken over as head coach, and he had a history of winning. But Jim Tressel also had a testimony that impressed Jay. Winning was important, but it wasn't everything. And Jay learned many important lessons about how to live life because he played for Coach Tressel for those four years.

I have been amazed at the opportunities that Jay has received through football. Many people told me that I was lucky to have a son playing for Ohio State. I don't believe in luck. I believe in God. I believe that everything that happens occurs for a particular purpose and is part of God's plan for our lives, including dreams. God gives us dreams so that we have a purpose in life, so that we can make a difference in the world. The Bible is right: without dreams, people are as good as dead. But through their dreams, God will provide opportunities for our children to do amazing things.

Nurturing the Dream
As parents, we all want to see our children experience those amazing things.

But let me be very clear here: dreams alone are not enough. There is no overnight success, only hard work and preparation. Someone once said that luck is where preparation meets opportunity—and the harder you work, the luckier you'll become. No child will reach his full potential without effort. She will have to work hard and have the wisdom to make the right choices that will eventually lead to her destiny.

And that is where you as a parent come in.

You have a role to play in whether or not your child will be able to reach his dreams. You need to be ready to steer your child through the sand traps, detours, successes and failures of following her dream. You will need a plan, a dream team, priorities, and a whole lot of patience. And I'm going to talk about each of those things (and a few others) in the rest of this book.

But before I do, I need to introduce you to two principles that are the heart of my advice for sports parents. Every chapter that follows draws upon these two principles and offers practical insights for putting them into practice. But these two ideas are the foundation—they are absolutely vital to a successful athletic experience for both you and your student.

1. Above all else, you are a sports PARENT.

Throughout my many years of involvement in athletics, this is the principle I have seen most often ignored or overlooked. Unfortunately, you will never be a successful sports parent if you emphasize the *sports* over the *parenting*.

We must take seriously our role as the parents of our children. And a parent's job is, first of all, to nurture their child's dream. To put it into athletic terms, a parent is a dream coach.

A coach teaches the skills and strategies that will make your child successful on the field. And what the coach does on the field, we do for every other area of our children's lives. We cannot focus only on encouraging their dreams of playing a sport (or learning an instrument or fixing cars or whatever is in their heart to do). We also have the responsibility to teach them how to live so that they can reach those dreams. Our job is to nurture our child, through her participation in sports, to become all that she is meant to be.

Nurturing our children means supporting them completely. I was blessed with parents who nurtured my talents. No matter what I said I wanted to do or how much was involved, my mom always found a way to support me. Following her example, I determined to support my children, too. Each of my sons has required different kinds and amounts of support, but no matter what it took, I was absolutely committed to them. As a sports parent, your children need the same level of support from you.

Nurturing our student athletes also requires encouraging them. Praise them for every step forward, but be realistic. Encouragement must be genuine to be effective, so be honest with yourself and your children. In seventh grade, Jay wasn't the most talented player on the team, but I knew with the proper training he could be really good. Some days Jay would lament that someone was better than he was or that he didn't get to play as much as he wanted to, but I simply encouraged him to keep working to get better. I was careful to affirm Jay and his efforts, but I was just as careful not to communicate that he somehow deserved to skip the hard work that others had done to get where they were. As sports parents, we have to work hard to find that difficult balance.

Finally, nurturing our children means that we always do what is best for them. That doesn't sound difficult, but this is the area where many parents struggle the most.

Some parents actually tear down their children's dreams, keeping them from achieving what is in their hearts to do. We must avoid this trap at all costs. A dream can be very fragile at times, so we must respond carefully to our children's dreams. A dear friend shared the following poem with me when I was in high school.

He Wishes for the Cloths of Heaven
William Butler Yeats
Had I the heaven's embroidered cloths,
Enwrought with golden and silver light,
The blue and the dim and the dark cloths
Of night and light and the half-light,
I would spread the cloths under your feet:
But I, being poor, have only my dreams;
I have spread my dreams under your feet;
Tread softly because you tread on my dreams.

The point here is clear: dreams are precious treasures and must be treated with care and humility—especially by parents. Yes, dreams can be destroyed by negative influence, imbalance, or difficult circumstances, but it is a parent's response, more than any of these, that will affect a child's dreams. Never mock your child's dream or tell him that he'll never be good enough to reach it. Sports parents must remember to "tread softly" on their children's dreams, or we will do more harm than we can possibly imagine.

Other sports parents try to impose dreams on their children. We have all heard of parents who push their athletes to play or continue in a sport they do not love. Instead of living out a dream, these children simply burn out. As their parents keep pushing them to excel, the fun disappears. They become angry, depressed, even physically injured. The activity becomes a burden, and often, these kids lose their love of the sport altogether. Even as adults, they may carry resentment and frustration over a lost childhood.

Clearly, that kind of "stage parenting" is unhealthy. But there are other ways to impose dreams on our children, too. Instead of forcing a child to fulfill the parent's dream, some parents try to force their children to find a new dream. They want to redirect their children to an "acceptable" path because the child's dream seems too risky, too boring, or too insignificant.

In grade school, Jay had a really good friend and fellow teammate who was a tall athletic-looking young man. For years he played football with Jay, but after a while he stopped enjoying the game. He would often tell me that his dad wanted him to play for Ohio State, but that he was tired of playing football. His father was livid when he quit the team, and eventually the young man dropped out of high school and started working on cars. He loved working in the auto shop and became an accomplished mechanic. But, sadly, he is still living under the shadow of his dad's disappointment.

As sports parents, we cannot impose dreams on our children. We must let them follow their dreams, allow them to do what is best for them, even when we think we know a better way. Imposing dreams on our children leads to bitterness and discouragement, and we must guard against that impulse so that we can help our children become all that they were meant to become.

As sports parents, our first job is to nurture our children, not push them. But a dream coach has to do more than just nurture their child's dream. We must, secondly, treat our athletes as whole people, remembering that they are also students, friends, community members, and soon-to-be adults. In other words, being a dream coach is all about keeping perspective. The world of sports offers our students amazing opportunities to learn about life and how to manage it. So instead of being consumed with starting or winning, a good sports parent will see (and help her child to see) that a sport is much more than a game to be won.

For example, when I remarried and moved our family into a new school district, Jay insisted that he could not leave his friends and his teammates and move to the new school. I had more than one family offer to let Jay use their address so that he could remain in the school district. But I adamantly refused. I explained to Jay that not only was this against school policy, but he could also jeopardize his entire team by being dishonest. Even more importantly, it was against what the Bible said was right. I used that experience to remind Jay that he would be blessed by doing the right thing (Deuteronomy 11:27), and of course, that is exactly what happened. Changing schools provided opportunities for Jay that he would not have had at his previous school. It opened doors that otherwise would have been closed for him.

We also moved only four blocks away. At that same time, Jay had other friends who moved out of state. This, too, was an opportunity for a life lesson. I reminded Jay that, even though we had moved, he was at least close enough that he could still walk to see them. I told him that life would send him many such changes and how he handled each would determine how far he would go in everything he ventured to do in life.

Sports parents must remember that we are, first of all, *parents*. Yes, our children love sports. So do we. But we need to be their supporters, but not their friends. We need to have dreams for our children and encourage them to have dreams from themselves. But we must also "tread softly" so that we do not undermine the very goal we are trying to achieve: our children's success.

2. You are not alone

Being a sports parent can be a surprisingly lonely road. Many parents have shared with me about the moments when they felt that they were fighting for their child against an overwhelming sea of opposition. And I have been there, too.

Even after years of being a sports parent, I have been blindsided by those moments of isolation. When we arrived in Arizona to watch Ohio State play for the National Championship in 2002, I was shocked to find that there was absolutely no one to help the players' parents navigate the craziness surrounding the game. No shuttles, no itinerary, nothing. It was quite overwhelming at the time.

But that moment was also a spark, a starting point. In fact, without that moment, this book would never have been written. That day, I decided to act on the one reality that I have found to be true among sports parents: no matter how alone you may feel, sports parents are a community.

I learned about this community when Jay was in eighth grade. While on the sidelines during a game, I was hit by a player and ended up with a compound fracture in my ankle. It was three months before I was able to return to work or to another game. I knew I could rely on my boys, our family and some friends to help me until my ankle healed enough for me to do things myself. But I was not expecting any help from other sports parents.

At the time, I didn't know many of the families on Jay's team. Most of the boys had played together since elementary school, but we had only lived in our community for about three years, and I worked 25 miles away. However, these families provided amazing support for me and for my sons. They organized six weeks of meals and arranged for my boys to get to all of their activities. People

I hardly knew stopped by with bags of groceries and prepared meals.

That kind of support can only come from people who live the life you do. And that is the beauty of the sports parent community. Sports parents understand what other sports parents need. That is why, when we discovered during the National Championship game that there was no organization at Ohio State for parents of football players, I decided to create one. So I did. In 2002, we established The Football Parents Association to provide information and assistance to the parents of every football player at Ohio State.

Through that Association, I have connected with other parents, making sure they received the support and community they needed to best help their student navigate the world of college athletics at Ohio State. In addition, I've been privileged to reach out to sports parents through speaking opportunities, radio shows, and now, this book.

And it all started because a group of families came to my aid when I needed them the most. Being a sports parent is more than just watching your child playing a sport; it means being part of a group of caring people whose passion goes beyond the game. Find ways to connect to and participate in this community. You are not alone.

Finishing the Dream

I am a sports parent.

I have loved every second of steering my boys through the amazing and sometimes crazy world of athletics. Together, we have navigated various sports, innumerable coaches, injuries (mine as well as theirs), major accomplishments, minor setbacks, and the daily reality that is life when your student is an athlete. Over these years, I've gleaned valuable principles about what to do for my boys. I've also learned the hard way what not to do. I've heard from coaches what they wish parents and athletes knew, and I've watched countless other sports families walk through these lessons as well.

And I hope to share what I have learned with you.

Being a good sports parent can be difficult. It requires a little bit of trial and error. And it takes a whole lot of wisdom. So for the rest of this book, I will share with you some of the lessons I have learned. In the next six chapters, I want to offer you advice on how to be the best sports parent you can be. We will discuss how to be your child's advocate, how to make a plan, how to set the right priorities and how to connect with your student so that, together, you will be able to see his or her dreams become a reality.

Because it always starts with a dream.

Chapter Two

Become Your Child's Advocate.

"The child supplies the power but the parents have to do the steering." - Benjamin Spock

The Roles of the Sports Parent

When I say the phrase *sports parent*, what comes to mind?

For many people, "sports parent" is just another way of saying "stage parent." Their only image is of those fan-parents who come to every game dressed from head to toe in the team's colors and sporting their athlete's number on jerseys, earrings, scarves, even painted on their faces. For a lot of people, "sports parents" are the over-zealous parents who arrive first, leave last, and refuse to sit down—even for halftime!

Now, don't get me wrong. I have worn my son's number for events, games, even on my blog's homepage! So clearly, I am not opposed to blatant visual support of your athlete. But is that all the term "sports parent" should bring to mind? Is that primarily what being a sports parent is all about?

And of course, the answer is no.

Obviously, a sports parent is going to do a whole lot more than just sit in the stands during games and cheer. Yes, that is important. But it is not, by any means, all that a sports parent will do for his child.

No matter what sport a child plays, a sports parent must be prepared to function as a chauffeur, nurse, motivational speaker, publicity coordinator, personal therapist or practice facilitator. Sometimes all on the same day! When my sons were growing up, I was their counselor, prayer warrior, disciplinarian, proofreader, nurturer, teacher, and decision-maker—and frankly, I always wished for a personal assistant to help me keep up with it all!

But even though a sports parent will wear hundreds of hats over the years, one role is, without a doubt, the most important. No matter what else you do, the role that you must play is that of *advocate*. Nothing else you will do is as important as this one thing.

Athletes at all levels of competition need someone they know is in their corner. For professional athletes, this role is often filled by an agent. An agent markets his client. He facilitates communication and handles the athlete's PR. He provides input on professional decisions, and he is expected to be widely knowledgeable not only about the sport, but also about management, the media, and sound financial principles.

Of course, at the student level, a parent is not an agent. And I am certainly not suggesting that we need professional agents for peewee league sports teams. However, I firmly believe that no athlete will ever survive the ups and downs of the athletic world without this kind of support. Every athlete needs someone to be her advocate. And it is my challenge to sports parents to willingly take on that vital role in their student's life.

So what, exactly, does it mean to be an advocate for your student athlete?

Simply put, an advocate is one who speaks on behalf of or wholeheartedly supports a particular cause or person. An advocate counsels, defends, and protects someone else. As a sports parent, being your child's advocate means helping your child navigate the maze of experiences he will face while participating in his sport in order to ensure that he has a positive and rewarding experience that ultimately prepares him for life as an adult.

Sounds like a pretty big task, doesn't it? Well, it is. But despite how overwhelming that description may sound, you, as sports parent, are probably already doing much of what you need to do.

Me...An Advocate?

Think back to the moment your child first told you that he or she wanted to play a sport. You probably started by getting a crash course in the basics of that sport, but you also, in all likelihood, found your life suddenly consumed with helping your student survive and even thrive in the crazy world that is athletics.

You made sure he was on time for practices and games. You encouraged her to work hard in areas that didn't come naturally to her. You cheered for wins and cried over losses. You talked to the coach and other parents about how to assist your child at home. You sat through events in the rain and the cold. You may have even had to stand up for your son or daughter in the face of an unfair coach, an unkind parent, or that horribly blind referee.

In other words, you instantly became your child's advocate.

Most parents have simply never thought of themselves in these terms, but that is precisely why this chapter is here. As a sports parent, you have the unique ability—the background, commitment, and perspective—to be your child's advocate better than virtually anyone else.

Unfortunately, the ability to be an advocate doesn't always translate into actually *being* an advocate. Not every parent is willing to play this role. Sometimes, a parent wants to be an advocate, but simply cannot because of job requirements, family issues or other intruding realities. And I also realize that sometimes one (or more) parent is absent altogether from the child's life. As a single mom for a number of years, I know how hard it is to advocate for your children while simply trying to stay afloat.

Also, learning to be an advocate is not easy. Even for parents who are willing, there can be a steep learning curve. You will make mistakes. Like anything else in life, some aspects of advocating for your child will come more easily than others. But no matter how much work it takes, learning to play this role is the best way to help your student athlete succeed.

That's why, for the rest of this chapter, I want to give you some specific advice about what it means (and doesn't mean) to be an advocate so that you will be even better equipped to serve your athlete this way for as long as she continues in her sport.

What an Advocate is NOT

There are three primary roles that an advocate is not to play.

An advocate is not a COACH.
An advocate is not a FAN.
An advocate is not a FRIEND.

Clearly, I do not mean that a sports parent is never a fan, never a friend, never a coach. These roles are important. However, many sports parents believe that filling these roles is the same as being an advocate. And unfortunately, that is simply not the case.

First of all, an advocate cannot also be a coach.

Again, I do not mean to say that no parent should ever coach his or her child. Parents do a great deal of good when they step up to lead peewee football, little league, or youth soccer teams. It is also good for parents to practice with their children or help them create training regimens so that they can develop into better athletes.

But it is even more important that parents have clear boundaries.

The fact is, being an advocate means you will eventually need to draw a line between being your child's coach and being his advocate. A coach's responsibility is to win games; he is committed to seeing the entire team succeed. You, on the other hand, will need to position yourself to support the coach's vision, while still protecting your student's experience on and off the field. That is why you will need clear and intentional boundaries.

Sometimes those boundaries are very literal. The most important lesson I learned from breaking my ankle during Jay's eighth grade season was that I needed to give Jay space. During those three months of recovery, I realized that as much as I wanted be on the sidelines with my son, I was not his coach. It is best for my boys for me to keep a respectable distance while I gently champion their dreams. And the same is true for most sports parents. We must work with the coach, but we cannot stand too close to the action. A sports parent's place is in the stands unless he or she is obligated to be closer to the action (as my ankle can attest!).

But even in a not-so-literal sense, we must respect the boundaries that our children need. Sports parents can become so passionate that they get too close emotionally, and everyone must deal with the consequences of that connection. We often call this "helicopter" parenting, and usually, the intentions are quite good. Helicopter parents want to protect, to assist, to guarantee success.

But this lack of boundaries only leads to problems. The child cannot mature as he needs to. She cannot learn to be independent as she should. And many times, the athlete becomes overwhelmed, even smothered, by this level of attention. So sports parents must establish clear boundaries. No matter how good it feels to be close, we have to step back and let our children develop the skills they need to learn so that they can truly succeed.

Michael Thompson described the situation this way:

When you and your child share a natural gift—be it for sports, music, or math—it may seem logical to play coach. Managing the peewee soccer team is one thing, but few parents can guide their child's career to a high level without damaging their relationship. Parents already have so much power in their children's lives, to add the role of coach tips the balance in a way that puts a child's mental health at risk. I'll never forget the boy I knew who quit the varsity basketball team in his senior year just to punish his sports-mad father. "That's all he cares about in my life," the boy said. Wise parents turn the job of coaching over to someone else they trust.[1]

Being a coach is not the same thing as being an advocate. The coach can be a positive role model, but as an advocate, your influence extends to every area of your child's life, not just her sport. Yes, you should know what the coach is saying to your student. You do need to understand the coach's philosophy. You should support the coach as much as you can. But you also need to keep a respectful distance, from the coach and from your student, so that you can help your athlete navigate the rigors of athletics without losing sight of all that he can become in the rest of life.

Next, an advocate is not a FAN.

Living in Columbus, Ohio, fanaticism is something I understand very well. The Ohio State Buckeyes boast a fan base that is almost rabid in its devotion. No one better talk down about OSU in Columbus (or anywhere else, for that matter)! In fact, the whole city just about shuts down during Buckeye games!

And that is all fine and good for Ohio State football. But when a sports parent is a fan, instead of an advocate, two problems can develop. First, a fan will always lose sight of the big picture.

Fans have the luxury of being completely biased. They idolize their favorite team and player, sometimes admiring them to the point of ignoring their flaws. Their hero can hit better, throw farther, run faster. Their team is the absolute best, period.

An advocate, on the other hand, cannot afford to be blindly biased. Being an advocate means you cannot focus only on stats or win-loss records. You cannot be consumed solely with your child's performance on the court or field. An advocate has to balance what happens during the games with the rest of the student's life.

As parents, we should be our child's biggest supporter. We should enjoy watching our athletes do well on the field. We need to believe in them and cheer them on, but we also need to maintain a mindset that knows that one game or one season is not the ultimate reality. A fan may be destroyed by that season-ending loss, but an advocate always chooses to see the bigger picture.

The second problem with being a fan, instead of an advocate, is the tendency to be consumed by emotion, especially towards the coach.

No parent will like every decision a coach makes. He might move your son to a different position or bench him altogether. A coach might favor another athlete over your daughter or pull her from a game without warning. Eventually, a coach is going to say or do something that you and your child will not like.

At that moment, you must think like an advocate, not a fan.

Fans can become as rowdy and emotional as they want. They can fly off the handle and shout their frustration to the heavens. But as an advocate, you do not have that luxury.

An advocate has to control his emotions. Never badmouth the coach in front of your child. Instead, show your athlete how to respond to the coach with respect, no matter what.

If she is having a disagreement with the coach, encourage her to work it out directly with the coach. Have him discuss with the coach why a decision was made or what he can do to get better in the coach's eyes. Model respect, and then teach your student how to do the hard work of being respectful even when he or she may not feel like it.

If having your student initiate communication doesn't work, then you can step in to advocate for your child. Talk to the coach on your own. But again—model respect. Don't confront the coach in front of others or yell obscenities from the stands. A fan behaves that way, but for a parent, acting that way will embarrass your child and may even hurt his or her chances of resolving the conflict.

The fact is—a parent who is a fan, instead of an advocate, has the power to seriously damage her student's prospects. Our children become what we model for them, and if we model disrespect for our athletes, that's what they will learn. Unfortunately, if a student develops a habit of disrespecting coaches, it can keep him from playing at the next level. No coach is going to deal long-term with a player who has an attitude problem; a disrespectful athlete will always have a short career.

But surprisingly, even if the athlete has a good attitude, the parent's lack of respect can still negatively affect the athlete's prospects. One recent article on recruiting described a parent yelling and screaming at a coach because she didn't think her son had been properly utilized during the game. Unfortunately, a college coach was at that game to scout out the athlete, and when he saw the parent disrespecting the coach, he decided it was not a good idea to have that family on his team.[2]

As an advocate, you can never forget that what a parent does or says will affect your student athlete. It may feel good for a minute to let the coach know publicly how you feel about his coaching, but if this is the behavior you model for your child, it will adversely affect his attitude and his opportunities in the long run.

What the coach says must be respected, by you and by your athlete. You don't have to like everything the coach thinks or says about your child, but you must choose to be an advocate instead of a fan and respond well, no matter what.

Finally, an advocate is not a FRIEND.

Whether you want to admit it or not, being a parent is far more important for your child's future than being his or her friend. Your student will have lots of friends—

hopefully, good ones who help her towards her goal. But your role as parent, and as advocate, goes far beyond the influence of a friend.

The primary problem with being a friend instead of an advocate is that you focus on making your child happy above all else. When being a friend is the goal, you will worry far more about whether you have hurt his feelings or made her mad at you than about what habits she is developing and what kind of person he is becoming.

On the other hand, being an advocate means recognizing that sometimes it's okay to be the "bad guy" in order to see your child develop to the fullest of her potential.

Shortly after my middle son, Joshua Alexander, got his scholarship to Kansas University, he asked if he could go with a friend to a Little Sibs weekend at a college a few hours away. He told me that his friend had a sister at the school (though his friend had only ever told me about having a brother).

Because I didn't feel good about this situation and because Josh didn't have a sibling at the school, I did not let him go. I explained that he was on a good course to a great future and had too much at stake to hang out at a school where he could possibly get in trouble. Of course, he was not pleased with my answer, and he sulked for the rest of the day.

If we want to advocate well, we have to focus on more than just making our athletes happy. As parents, we must always keep in mind the bigger context for every request our students make. We will have to set boundaries and enforce them firmly. We will have to say "no" to some opportunities. We may have to ask our students to wait for something or refuse permission for something that they really want to do. In other words, we will have to be the "bad guy."

Obviously, it is never fun to say no. Knowing Josh was upset with me was not pleasant. But even though my decision didn't make him happy at first (he did admit later that he was glad I hadn't let him go), it was clearly the right choice for that particular instance. And that is the point. Our athletes won't always like our decisions, and it won't be easy to say no, but playing the bad guy when necessary is worth it in the long run.

Being an advocate instead of a friend also means allowing your child to fail when necessary. A child needs to learn, as early as possible, that failure is going to happen and that they are capable of dealing with it. As Robert Heinlein, an American novelist, once said, "Don't handicap your children by making life easy."

As scary as it seems, it really is all right to let your child mess up and face the consequences. Of course, you should never set her up to fail. But when the opportunity arises, let your student deal with the results of his decisions. This might mean not providing forgotten sports equipment and clothing. It could mean allowing her to make a decision that you believe is not the best. But your child will only benefit when, instead of fixing his mistakes for him, you help him work through the consequences of a mistake.

One morning, when Jay was in fifth grade, he missed the bus. He called me at work, wanting me to come home and take him to school. When I asked him how he missed the bus, he admitted he had been watching cartoons and time had gotten away from him. I could have come home to get him, but I decided that it was time for him to learn a lesson about being responsible. I told Jay to walk to school. He was outraged and told me it was too far to walk (it was about a mile away). I gave him 30 minutes to get to school or face the consequences. Then I called the principal, explained what I had done, and asked for a call when he had safely arrived.

That evening Jay was still angry with me. "You ought to be glad that I didn't get hit by a car!" He told me there were dead animals and trash on the road he had to travel to get to school. Obviously, it was not a pleasant experience for him, but he didn't miss the bus again.

Sometimes the best way to advocate for our athletes is to step out of the way and let them fall down. That way they will learn how to get back up. Dealing with the consequences of bad decisions will help your student learn to make wise decisions. And a small dose of failure, with you there to help her through it, will enable your student to deal with the difficult and sometimes painful experiences that life will hold for her in the future.

It might not be fun, but it will always be worth it.

What an Advocate DOES do

So an advocate cannot be merely a coach, a fan, or a friend. But what, then, should an advocate do? To advocate well, a parent needs to focus on four primary roles.

An advocate is an ALLY.
An advocate is INVOLVED.
An advocate is a MANAGER.
An advocate has a PLAN.

First of all, being an advocate means being your child's ALLY.

To be an ally is to be your student's champion. It means letting your child know that you are for her, that you care about what he says and does. It means that your children know that your love is unconditional, that nothing they do can change how you feel about them.

Of course, this is a basic tenet of good parenting, but it's absolutely vital for sports parents. A student athlete works and plays hard, all the while hoping to see his parents' approval. Even if it doesn't always seem that way, your student doesn't want to let you down. And he needs to know you love him—win or lose, success or failure, no matter what.

As a mom of three student athletes, I constantly tried to let my boys know that there was nothing they could do to make me stop loving them. They knew that I believed in them and would stand behind them. And while I did not always approve of their actions, that didn't change my support for them. Even when my sons' actions or attitudes displeased me, I made it a point to be supportive, while I also dealt with their behavior.

Truly, there is no greater gift we can offer our athletes. I recently saw a video featuring Shawn Johnson, the former Olympic gymnast, and her mother. Over and over, Shawn emphasized her mom's complete support throughout her career. When Shawn seriously considered leaving gymnastics, her mom refused to pressure her, promising to support her decision either way. That unconditional love and support gave Shawn the freedom to choose, and she decided to keep competing—because she actually wanted to.[3]

That is what it means to be your child's advocate, to be her ally. No matter what decision he makes, your student needs to know you'll stand with him. She needs to believe, without a doubt, that you are her biggest supporter, that you want her to follow her dreams.

Of course, that kind of support doesn't mean being unrealistic. Not every dream comes true, and you must always remember that encouraging and supporting your student is not the same as being untruthful.

Think about it. Statistically, your child has a one in 10 million chance of becoming president. Her odds of winning an Oscar: 11,500 to 1. The odds of winning an Olympic medal: 662,000 to 1.4 And the chances of your son playing in the NFL: 22,000 to 1.5 Those are not good odds.

Simply put, your child probably won't compete in the NFL or the Olympics. And that's okay. But as his advocate, you, of all people, must be real with your child. Be honest about his ability and his potential, and help to keep him grounded. Of course, that doesn't necessarily mean discouraging him from his dream. You don't have to tell her she can't succeed. Instead, simply explain the obstacles. Make sure she understands exactly what it will take to reach her goal. Then, if he is still determined to go for it, do everything you can to help him along the way. Encouraging a child to follow a dream doesn't guarantee it will come true, but a parent should support that child as long as the dream is his.

So, you must first be your child's ally. Secondly, you need to be INVOLVED—in everything.

Notice, however, that I did not say in control. Being an advocate is not the same as being a dictator. Many sports parents make every decision for their student. They decide which sport. They decide which coach. They push their student to higher levels and greater accomplishments, even after the athlete has lost the desire to continue. Dictators are so consumed with the student's performance that they often miss out on the person they are forcing their child to be.

Being an advocate, on the other hand, means being involved in your student's life without trying to control it. Make decisions together and give him freedom to determine what he does or does not want to do. Avoid criticizing her ideas; instead, offer feedback and advice so that she has all the information she needs to make a good choice. Then support her decision wholeheartedly.

For me, this principle was most important when my sons were choosing their sports. Going into seventh grade, Jay did not intend to try out for football. His passion, at the time, was basketball. While I did keep the option of football in front of him, if he had determined on that first day of school that he did not want to try out, I would have given him the freedom to make that choice.

Both of my other sons then had to determine whether or not to follow Jay into football. Joshua Alexander did eventually go that route. For Joshua Odis, on the other hand, football was not a perfect fit, and he eventually discovered his passion on the track team. For each of my boys, it was vital that I give them advice and feedback, but leave the final decision up to them.

This kind of involvement is also necessary when your child is dealing with outside input, especially from coaches, recruiters or the media. As an advocate, you need to position yourself so that you know what things are being said to your student. Again, this is not about controlling those conversations or forcing everyone to talk to you instead of your student, but you do need to dialogue with your child about outside feedback or offers. Communication is vital. You need to know what your student thinks about the offers being made, the advice being given, the commentary others are making. And you need to offer your own input both to validate and, at times, correct the responses your student is having.

Third, an advocate needs to act as the child's MANAGER, even from childhood.

As your child's advocate, you need to manage every aspect of his life: sports, academics and personal growth. I learned this truth when our youngest, Joshua Odis, started school. We didn't realize it at the time, but Odis is dyslexic. For the first few years of school he really struggled, but his teachers didn't seem concerned about his inability to recognize words. They suggested that he might just be a slow learner. I took him for a complete physical, and his doctor, too, told me not to worry about it.

Still, I knew in my heart something was not right. I knew his issues were not normal; I could see that he was very intelligent, but still struggled to learn. Finally, in third grade, I determined to get him some help. I prayed without ceasing for a solution. I researched the laws about accommodating children with learning differences, and I found a school that would evaluate him. I took all of this information to Odis' school and insisted that they either find an appropriate system to teach him to read or pay for the other school (where tuition was $40,000 a year). Needless to say, the school quickly found a system that worked for Odis. He was reading by the next year, and by the time he reached high school, he was taking AP courses.

These results were not magic or luck. Things changed because I realized my son needed my help. I pursued a solution, and once we had a plan, I became the manager of that plan to make sure we all stayed on track.

Of course, Odis' dyslexia primarily affected his academic progress, but the same principles apply to athletics as well. We must learn to manage our students' experiences. Again, I am not talking about *micro*managing your child's life. A manager is not a diva parent who controls and manipulates the child. Instead, an advocate seeks to steer the child in the direction that is most beneficial to that child in the long run, no matter what the teachers or coaches may say.

When Olympic gymnast Shawn Johnson was about eight, her coach began pushing to have Shawn moved to the next level of competition. She was clearly good enough to move up, but instead of just letting it happen, Shawn's mother requested that Shawn be kept at the lower level. She didn't want Shawn to be pushed ahead so fast that she stopped enjoying her sport. She let the coach provide recommendations, but always pursued what was best for Shawn overall. That is what it means to be a true manager.[6]

Sadly, that attitude is not the norm. For most sports parents, whatever the coach recommends is the right path. They simply follow his lead. But these parents forget that *they* need to be the biggest influence in their child's life. And the consequences of this mistake can be significant.

I knew of one high school coach who told a tenth-grader that he'd never be big enough to play college ball. The student was so discouraged that he quit the team. Sadly, he is now a tall, athletic man in his twenties, but he missed his chance to pursue college football. That same coach told another boy the same thing—he was too small to play Division I football; but thankfully, that young man's parents refused to take that as the final word. They told their son that he could be whatever he wanted to be if he worked hard enough. That young man is now on a Division I football team.

Being a parent, being an advocate, means choosing to be the driving force in your child's life, rather than letting the coach be the one directing the entire show. Obviously, you should take into account what your child's coach is saying. But you cannot rely on the coach to decide what should happen or to make sure that it actually happens. As a manager, you have to take your student's circumstances and make them work for your child and the dream he or she hopes to achieve.

I learned this lesson when our second son, Joshua Alexander, was in high school. Jay had been heavily recruited for scholarships, but for Joshua it was different. He is as gifted as Jay, but he doesn't have the same build. In ninth grade, he had the frame and the desire to play well, but he still struggled. Week after week, I watched him during football games and at track meets, wondering when it was going to click. Finally, it did, and in tenth grade, he set the school record for high jump and long jump and lettered in football.

But even though he lettered in football, he was not where he wanted to be. He wanted desperately to be a receiver, but the coach had him playing end and linebacker. At one point I talked to the coach myself, and he told me he had someone else in mind and that Josh had a better chance to start at safety.

As Josh's manager, I had a choice to make. I wasn't happy with the coach's decision, but I refused to moan and complain about the coach to my son. Instead, I adjusted my own plan. Of course, I thought he would make a great receiver, but I also knew he couldn't make plays sitting on the bench. So I encouraged him to be the best possible safety he could be, and that's exactly what he did. Ironically, he also discovered that he really enjoyed hitting. And the change eventually paid off. In his senior year Josh got the award for the most improved player and was offered a full scholarship to Kansas University.

As an advocate, you are your child's manager. The coach must do what is best for the team, but your focus is much bigger. You have to take the coach's decisions or recommendations and use them to help your athlete achieve his or her dreams.

Finally, an advocate has to have a PLAN.

Having a plan is absolutely vital to the pursuit of your athlete's goal. It is a step that cannot be missed, and it is so significant, that I'm going to spend the entire next chapter discussing how to craft such a plan for your child.

For now, however, just keep in mind that your student needs you to be her ally. You need to be involved, offering support and encouragement. You need to manage her experiences, in athletics and in life. Together, you and your student will need to formulate a plan that will take him where he wants to go. By making these four areas your highest priorities, you will ensure that your student always has the support he needs to reach his dreams. You will be an advocate.

One Final Thought: Advocate for Others, Too

Before we head to the next chapter and discover how to make a plan for your child, however, there is one last idea that I need to share. As I mentioned before, all students need an advocate, someone they know is on their side.

However, there are many children who have a love for sports but no committed parents to help them realize their dream. If your child no longer has a desire for sports or if they never develop the desire to play, please consider supporting another student athlete. Check with your school's athletic association, AAU or coaches in the area to identify a player who could use a cheerleader and volunteer your time and support. It may not be the same as seeing your child on the field, but your support will enable that child to grow into a successful adult.

Even with my own three boys to support, I have had many opportunities to do exactly this. One of the most memorable students came to me while I was substitute teaching in the inner city. Having grown up in inner-city Cleveland, I know how important it is to give back to students who may not get all the encouragement that they need, so I took every opportunity I could to build up students who lacked a good support system.

One day I was covering a social studies class when a very athletic looking young man came to the room and asked if I was that "football lady." I told him I was, and he asked if he could talk with me about a problem he was having. He told me that he had a good grade point average (well over a 3.0), but a low ACT score. He was now ready to re-take the test to try for a higher score, but unfortunately, he had used his only voucher to take the exam and now needed $38 or a credit card. He didn't have either one, and no one in his family could or would provide the money for him. He was a talented student-athlete who had done all he needed to do to become eligible for a scholarship only to have $38 get in the way. I gladly paid the exam fee; he got the needed score, was recruited for a college scholarship, and became the starting running back on his team.

It was a blessing for me to play a small role in helping that young man achieve his dream. My small contribution gained me another son of whom I am so proud, but there are many other students out there just like him. Every student deserves an advocate, and I highly recommend that you consider offering your support in situations just like these.

There is immense power in being an advocate for a child, your own and for others. You can be a voice for the children who cannot speak effectively for themselves. You can enable them to achieve more than they could possibly do on their own. You don't have to be a perfect parent, but you do need to give all that you have towards being your child's advocate, on and off the field.

Endnotes:

1. Michael Thompson, "Flying Solo" May 2012, Parents. 10 Oct. 2012 <http://www.parents.com/kids/responsibility/teaching/raise-independent-child/?page=1>

2. "The Impact of Crazy Helicopter Parents During the Athletic Recruiting Process," Recruiting-101.com, 2012. 12 Nov. 2012 <http://recruiting-101.com/the-impact-of-crazy-helicopter-parents-during-the-athletic-recruiting-process/>

3. "Raising an Olympian - Shawn Johnson," Online video clip, YouTube , 7 May 2012. 25 Sept. 2012 <http://www.youtube.com/watch?v=ULHXOz9Wk2M>

4. "The Odds #1," Funny2.com, 2012. 25 Sept. 2012. <www.funny2.com/odds.htm>

5. Jay Richardson, 2012, The Jay Richardson Foundation. 25 Sept. 2012 <www.thejayrichardsonfoundation.org/aboutus.htm>

6. "Raising an Olympian." <http://www.youtube.com/watch?v=ULHXOz9Wk2M>

Chapter Three
Mapping the Path: Creating Plan A (and B)

Commit to the Lord whatever you do and your plans will succeed. Proverbs 16:3

The Path to Success

H.L. Hunt was a very successful man. Nearly bankrupt in 1930, he was one of the wealthiest men in the world when he died in 1974. When asked how he had managed that kind of success, H.L. Hunt offered this advice, "Decide what you want, decide what you are willing to exchange for it. Establish your priorities and go to work."

As a sports parent, I love Mr. Hunt's perspective on success. No matter what sport your child plays, success is the goal. Each player wants to win the game, the championship, the medal. The desire for success is always part of the reason that an athlete competes.

But success is not guaranteed. For every Olympian who takes home a gold medal, there are dozens more who miss out, sometimes by only a tenth of a second. In sports, someone has to win, and someone has to lose. Someone gets the scholarship and another does not. An injury, a coaching change, an unwise decision—all it takes is one second, one phone call, one bad call, and an athlete's hope of achieving success lies shattered on the ground.

That's why I am amazed by the success with which God has blessed my sons. Having all three of my boys achieve the levels of accomplishment that they have is astounding. Many people will say to me, "You are so lucky to have two sons with Division I scholarships and a son in the NFL." But are they just lucky? Or is there something more?

Obviously, success requires more than luck. But even hard work and passion are not enough. Certainly, your athlete needs to have the desire to succeed (that's the dream we talked about in Chapter 1). But she can want it more than anyone else, work harder than anyone else, and still never reach the top. No, your child needs something to go along with his passion, to give direction to his effort.

He needs a plan.

I am convinced that success only comes through planning, preparation, good direction and the grace of God. If I had just wished for my boys to get scholarships, but didn't plan and work hard, it would not have happened. Like H.L. Hunt, we had to decide what we wanted and then figure out how we were going to get there. The same will be true for you and your student athlete.

An Individual Plan

You and your athlete need a plan. You need a personal strategy for success. Together, you need to map out the path that you intend to pursue in order to achieve his or her dream.

Thankfully, what I am talking about here is not complicated. It does not have to be professional. It is not going to be permanent. But in order for it to be effective, there are two things that your plan must be.

First, it must be *unique* to your athlete.

There are many different ways to fulfill a particular dream. To earn a Division I scholarship, for example, some athletes spend extra time in practice. Others focus on making contacts and attending recruiting camps. No two athletes will follow the same path to a particular goal, so the plan you create with your child is really relevant only to your child. Thus, it must be based entirely on your child's strengths, weaknesses, and goals.

Even in the same family, each student needs a unique plan. When Jay determined that he truly wanted to play college football, we started by crafting a plan. He was being recruited by schools all over the nation, so most of our plan for Jay involved identifying what he really wanted from the school of his choice and narrowing down the list to the top five schools we wanted to focus on.

But Joshua Alexander competed in both track and football for a while, and I was sure his scholarship would be for track. When he announced that he really wanted to play college football, we had to take a totally different approach. We had to create a resume that would help recruiters visualize him on their team. Our focus was also different. We knew we needed only one D-1 scholarship offer to see his dream come true, and finding that school became our goal. This process was not any less work than Jay's plan had required, but it was a completely different experience.

Finally, when Joshua Odis determined his path, we needed yet another plan. Joshua Odis was also on the track team, but had no interest in playing sports at the collegiate level. His dream is to get a degree in marketing and eventually start his own business, so we had to look for academic scholarships and financial plans to support his goals.

There is no such thing as "one plan fits all." I had to sit down with each of my sons, individually, to determine what he really wanted to do and what he had to do to make that happen. And clearly, each plan was very unique.

Getting Good Directions
Second, your plan needs to be *specific*.

An effective plan is always as detailed as possible. Think about it like driving directions. Good directions are very specific. Turn right here. Go 6.87 miles and merge slightly to the left. Expect your trip to take 3 hours and 14 minutes. Follow the plan, and you get where you want to go.

On the other hand, vague directions are simply not helpful. Someone trying to get from Columbus, OH, to Pasadena, CA, would need much better directions than these:
- Drive west until you leave Ohio.
- Keep driving west until you reach California.
- Stop when you arrive in Pasadena.

To be fair, these directions are accurate. You need to do all of those things to get from Ohio to Pasadena. But accurate is not the same thing as specific. And if you are trying to get from Point A to Point B, what you need is *specific*.

A plan for your student's athletic dream works the same way. You will need to be specific about the dream itself as well as the steps required to get there. Like those directions to Pasadena, if your plan is vague or uncertain, it will not get you where you want to go.

I tried very hard to impress this truth on my boys. It was important that they understand that dreams required work and planning. They don't just happen. So when one of my sons told me what he wanted to do, I asked questions about what was required and pointed out what they would have to do to make that dream to come true. Even when a dream seemed far-fetched, I refused to blow it off as impossible, but instead pointed out the specific actions they would need to take to make it happen.

I do realize, however, that being specific is not always easy. In fact, being specific can be downright scary. When you write down what you want and how you intend to get there, you suddenly realize all the obstacles in the way. You suddenly have to face questions like, "What if I can't do those things? What if I do all of this and still don't reach my dream?" Seeing the details forces you to decide how committed you really are to pursuing this crazy path.

But as difficult as it can be, being specific is essential to success. Your plan doesn't have to be perfect. It can and will change (more on that at the end of the chapter). But you must have a plan with clear and workable steps that can be followed, crossed off, or modified, if necessary. It is the only way you (and your student) will ever achieve your dreams.

So, exactly how do you write a specific plan?

One very helpful strategy that I have used is the SMART mnemonic. SMART stands for

- **S**pecific
- **M**easurable
- **A**ttainable
- **R**elevant
- **T**ime-bound

Focusing on these five qualities will ensure your plan is specific. It works like this. Instead of having your athlete write a goal to "Get better as a defensive end for next year," it is more effective to say, "By the end of next year's football season, I will have 4 sacks and 45 tackles."

The numbers make this goal specific. It is also measurable; he can keep track of sacks and tackles easily. It is attainable, though it may require extra preparation and practice. It certainly is relevant. And it is time-bound; the athlete has the entire season to work toward this goal. So by using the SMART tool, the athlete can create a very well-written plan.

Obviously, it might take some practice to learn to write goals this way. But the effort is well worth it; the pay-off will be more than you can imagine.

The Plan: A How-To

So, your student's plan needs to be unique and specific. But how do you create such a plan? Well, let's get practical. Here's a simple list to help you start the actual process of creating a plan for your student:

1. Do Research
2. Break it Down
3. Write it Down
4. Work Hard
5. Never Give up

Research

The first step to creating a good, specific plan with your student is to do your research. Read anything you can on your child's sport. Talk to coaches and other parents. Learn everything you possibly can about what is involved in your child's dream and what he or she will need to do to reach it.

Even more importantly, make sure that your child is doing research as well. When Joshua Alexander was five, he came home from school all excited about being an archaeologist. When I asked him what an archaeologist did, he replied, "They dig!" Needless to say, I took him to the library that evening, and we got books on archaeology.

Of course, he was five, and every few months he had a new dream. So every few months, we made another trip to the library. But the point is simple. No one can make plans for an area that they know nothing about. If your student wants to be a writer, a starting wide receiver, or an Olympic figure skater, make sure he or she knows what following that passion will entail. Work together and do your research.

Break it Down

No matter how big or overwhelming a dream might seem as a whole, it can be achieved when you divide it into smaller, more manageable steps. You and your student will need to break down his or her dream into segments. His ultimate goal may be to play professional football, but that dream cannot begin until he makes the Varsity team. Then he'll need to be recruited to play college football as well. These are smaller steps that he needs to pursue to reach his ultimate dream of playing professionally.

And each of those smaller segments has to be broken down into its own set of detailed goals. Making the Varsity team might mean setting goals for weight lifting or committing to 45 minutes of extra practice on his own every night after team practice. Earning a College scholarship may require setting goals for his GPA or for developing more speed on the field.

Simply put, once you have the big picture, work with your student to divide his big dream into workable sections so that you can plan effectively for each stage.

Write it Down

This step is absolutely essential. It must happen. Even if you are not, by nature, a list-maker, you and your child need to write on paper both the dream itself and the steps that must be accomplished to get there. You can cross off goals that have been reached and add new ones as needed. But a plan must be written down.

It is also vital that the plan be written by the person who has the dream. You cannot write a plan and hand it to your student to complete. You can (and should) suggest goals for your children, but ultimately they have to develop the goals that will support their plans. They need to think their dreams through and determine what steps they can and are willing to do in order to reach those goals. If all they do is write down the goals you suggest, but aren't really committed to them, those goals will not be accomplished.

I regularly encouraged my boys to write down their goals so that they could mark their progress as they realized each one. I wasn't always sure they were getting it, but I never stopped reminding them of this vital step. Then one morning I walked into Joshua Alexander's room and there, taped on his mirror, were his goals. I was so happy I wanted to cry. He had learned the benefit of writing down what he wanted and how to get there. And it has proven to be a valuable tool that he has used over and over as he has pursued his dreams, on and off the field.

Work Hard

Of course, writing down our dreams and goals will not accomplish anything unless we actually do the things we've written down. Dreaming about playing in the NFL is fine. It is important to keep the big picture in mind, but we must also encourage our student to do his or her best in the stage where he or she is right now. Reaching a goal means setting good goals and then *getting them done* by working hard.

The key to working hard is to dream big, but take small steps to get there. If your child's goal is to be on the honor roll, encourage him to take good notes and do his homework every day. With practice, he will develop good study habits that will result in good grades on tests and papers. And those grades will land him on the honor roll.

The same is true for an athletic goal. During Joshua Odis's first year in track, I would ask him how far he threw, and he would usually reply, "I don't know. I forgot to ask." I told him that he needed to pay attention to what was going on right then—his technique and what his results were—so he could determine how to get better. He didn't do well that first season, but during his second year, he decided to make some changes. He started keeping track of his throws and was encouraged by his progress. He practiced his technique and got progressively better. By junior year he lettered in track (shotput and discus) and was a leader on the team by senior year. By taking small steps and working hard, he developed into an accomplished athlete.

And obviously, crossing each step off the list will take time. Joshua Odis's success did not come overnight. Working hard means not getting ahead of yourself. It means encouraging your student to focus on the small things she can do every day. Those little habits become the foundation from which he'll be able to do bigger things. Getting too focused on the big dream often leads to discouragement and burn out. But if your student achieves little goals every day, she will be able to reach her dreams—no matter how big they are!

Never Give Up

Dream big. Take small steps. And never, ever give up.

No dream will ever be reached if we quit partway through. You need to encourage your student to keep trying, no matter how desperate things look right then. There will be hard moments where it seems that she can go no further. There may be times where difficulties appear that no one could have anticipated. But no matter what, you cannot give up.

Joshua Alexander learned this lesson the hard way. He dreamed of playing Division I football but didn't get any offers for a long time. So he worked hard on the field, getting better at his position until he was a starter with good stats. Then when he had met all of his football goals, he revised his plan for off-field activities. He began to write letters and visit more campuses. At one point, he even got with his team's quarterback in 30 degree weather to film himself running receiver routes so that he would have more film to offer prospective coaches. He refused to give up, no matter how many months went by without an offer, and he pursued his goals until he achieved his ultimate dream—playing Division I football.

The Bible says, "Write the vision and make it plain so that he that reads it can run with it" (Habakkuk 2:2). When we teach our children how to write clear goals and then encourage them to pursue those goals without giving up, there is nothing that will stop them from being successful.

A Parent's Plan

Every student needs a unique and specific plan in order to reach his or her goals. But it is vitally important for parents to have a plan, too.

This is not about having a plan *for* your kids. Yes, when my boys were really young, I had big plans for them. But as they developed a vision of their own, my dreams had to take a backseat. No matter what I dreamed for my boys, they had to want it for themselves to make it come true. They were not going to give their best to someone else's dream.

So a parent's plan is not about your children. Instead, you must write a plan for yourself. Every time I sat down with my boys to write or revise their plans, I also wrote down what I was going to do to support them in those plans. The same needs to be true for you. You need to be developing a specific and unique plan to define how you can best support your child's dreams.

There are two primary reasons for creating a parent's plan.

First, crafting a plan for yourself is a great way to model for your student the importance of always having a plan. When they watched me write down my plan, they could see that I was doing exactly what I was asking them to do. Writing a personal plan emphasizes for our children that we really do value setting goals and then working hard to reach them.

And second, having a plan for ourselves will help us create and maintain clear boundaries. Writing down in detail your role as a parent helps you support their dream without taking it over. You will be able to work in cooperation with your athlete, but you (and your student) will also have a well-defined separation between what you will do and what she must do for herself. Such a division of responsibilities is essential to teaching our students how to step up and work towards their goals. It forces them to take responsibility, and it forces us, as parents, to step aside so that they can do exactly that.

Clearly, it is just as valuable for you as a sports parent to have a clear and detailed plan as it is for your student. A parent's plan is another simple tool that will take you both one step closer to achieving your dreams.

A Change in Plans
Of course, you and your athlete can write brilliantly specific, well-crafted plans and cross each goal off as it is

reached. You can move closer and closer to your goal...only to have it fall to pieces right in front of your face.

The honest, and very difficult, truth is that our plans will not always succeed. Despite our best efforts, our Plan A can suddenly fall apart.

Sometimes, our plans fail for reasons far outside of our control. A new coach doesn't choose your son as a starter. No scholarships are offered, or an offer is suddenly withdrawn. An injury or accident knocks your daughter out for an entire season. A more talented athlete moves into the district, or your family suddenly has to move out. Any number of obstacles can present themselves, without warning, and each occurrence necessitates a change in plans.

On the other hand, our plans can also fall apart for very personal reasons. Your student may decide to pursue a new dream. He may choose a college that didn't offer him a scholarship. She may decide that her sport's time commitment is no longer worth the sacrifices.

But regardless of what circumstances arise, there may come a moment when you and your athlete suddenly need a new strategy, a new plan.

Moving to Plan B
So...what will you do then?

You will have to adjust your plans. You will have to find a new way through the difficulty. You will need a Plan B.

Obviously, making the shift to Plan B can be difficult. But it doesn't have to be. If you find yourself suddenly having to switch paths, you can make the transition as seamless as possible with a few simple steps.

Be Flexible.

First of all, both athlete and parent must stay flexible. When facing an unexpected turn of events, it is easy to get upset, uptight and refuse to budge. We want to rant and rave about the coach's decision. We sulk and struggle, trying to hold on to the original dream. But instead of trying to force the world back into the way it "used to be," choose to be flexible. Admit your disappointment and let your student express his as well. Then begin looking for new ways forward.

Be Creative.

Don't box yourself in. When creating a Plan B, look at all possibilities, even the far-fetched ones. Don't rule out any avenue until you've thought it through. Ideally, we would think about Plan B before we need it, but in most cases, that does not happen. So when you are faced with a sudden crisis, be willing to try new and different ideas to find a new path to the goal you want to reach.

Be Positive.

Absolutely nothing beats a positive attitude. You cannot control what circumstances life throws at you, but you can control your response to it. While it is not always easy, if you stay upbeat and look for new opportunities, you will be more than equipped to succeed.

I learned this lesson watching my son's best friend, Thomas. Thomas was a very talented athlete. He played several sports, but his dream was to be a football star. Unfortunately, at the end of his freshmen year, Thomas was diagnosed with a heart condition that required him to have open heart surgery. He had a wonderful recovery but was told that he could never play football again. Obviously, he was terribly disappointed. But he did not let this setback stop him. Thomas took his passion for running and put it to great use on the track team. By senior year, he placed second in the state for the 400 meter event and got a scholarship to a prestigious Division I track program.

Though it was not his first choice, his Plan A, Thomas stayed positive and flexible. He creatively used his talents in a different arena, and still found the athletic success that he enjoyed. Thomas is a perfect example of how to create a workable "Plan B."

Your student needs a plan, a strategy to get herself from right now to the fulfillment of her dream. And you can support your athlete by helping her manage this vital ingredient to success. Help him prepare for the detours and rough terrain along the way. Carefully work together to create a "Plan A," but be prepared to find a "Plan B" if necessary. Encourage your student to write down what he wants to accomplish and how he intends to get there and then encourage him to start pursuing that goal.

The old saying is right—the journey of a thousand miles really does begin with one step..

Chapter Four
Eligible Isn't Enough

Train up a child in the way he should go and when he is old he will not depart from it. Proverbs 22:6

Finding the Target

I always hoped my sons would be able to earn a college scholarship. I was convinced a scholarship was the best way to ensure that they would get the education I wanted them to have. And thankfully, earning a scholarship was an important goal for them, as well. Each of my sons worked hard to earn a good scholarship to a good school, and we have been blessed to see their efforts rewarded every time.

Of course, the dream of a college scholarship is a common one. Most sports parents love the idea of a free education for their children, and many athletes also have this objective as a specific part of their plan. Every goal they set—to practice harder, to become a starter, to develop each skill—is a small step toward the moment when they get the letter (or phone call) offering them a scholarship.

But getting a college scholarship is not necessarily an easy task. Which is why one of the most common questions that parents ask me is: "What do I need to do for my student to be eligible for a college scholarship?"

And my answer just might surprise you.

Eligible IS Important

To begin, let me be very clear. Making sure that your student is eligible for a scholarship is definitely important. His or her talent must be developed in order for there to be any hope that recruiters will come calling. You and your athlete need to spend the necessary time and energy to ensure that he or she meets all the physical requirements for eligibility in every level of the sport or competition. Together, you must focus on this goal.

Having shepherded my sons through the process, I can tell you that becoming eligible (and staying that way) takes a lot of work on your athlete's part. Talent must be nurtured. Your son needs to push himself to be the best baseball player he can be. Your daughter needs to practice her free throws every day. Simply put, scholarship offers only come with hard work and practice.

But sports parents also have a part to play. You will have to focus on the sport your child plays. You will commit money, time, and energy in ever-increasing amounts. I know. I was always involved alongside my sons in their athletic pursuits, whether on the sidelines or through athletic boosters and alumni associations. Without a doubt, eligibility requires a family focus.

The desire to see your student become eligible is good. You both need to focus on that goal, pursuing it rigorously and doing whatever you can to make it happen.

Eligible Isn't Enough
With all of that said, however, there is another side of the story.

Ensuring our athletes have developed their athletic abilities enough that they are eligible for scholarships is important. But it is not, by any means, the *most* important thing. As advocates for our students, we need to be most concerned they are well-rounded human beings, and not just superstar athletes.

The key word here is *balance*. Each student athlete needs to have a balanced focus. She needs a perspective that sees eligibility as only one part of who she is, and not necessarily the most important part.

Really, it's all about potential.

Dictionary.com defines potential as "possible as opposed to actual." Myles Munroe, a gifted theologian, describes potential as "all you can do but have not yet done."[1] We are born with exponential potential, but of course, if that potential is not nurtured, trained, properly restrained and polished, it is worth nothing.

As parents and advocates, we must make sure that we hone our child's **full** potential. What good is it for a student to be the fastest person on the team, but to have such low grades she can't compete? What good a starting quarterback whose test scores are so low he doesn't meet college entrance requirements? These students have developed their potential in one area, but neglected everything else. And the result is that **all** of their potential is wasted, even in the area where they worked so hard to succeed.

We would never put an incredible engine in a rusted-out car without oil or gas. All of that speed would go to waste. And the same is true for our children. Focusing only on talent is a waste of their potential. Only an athlete who is properly trained, both on *and* off the field, will be in any position to maximize her talent, to reach her full potential.

But how do we make sure our child is finding balance? We have to focus on three key areas.

First, as I've said, we do need to focus on our child's *talent*. An athlete's talent needs to be nurtured and trained in order for him to succeed. But we must also keep in perspective that talent alone is rarely enough. Other players can and will be better than our children. Injuries can and do happen. Obstacles of all kinds will arise, and our athletes will have to face the reality that, in the big picture, running a 4.6 forty yard dash doesn't guarantee success.

As parents and advocates, we must broaden our perspective, and we must help our students develop their talent without forgetting to prioritize two other key areas as well.

Hitting the Books
The first of these other areas is *education*. There is a difference between being eligible and being educated. Being eligible is a student getting the minimum grades required to qualify to participate in activities. Being educated means giving our children a full range of knowledge so they can compete in life and truly excel. And

understanding that difference is crucial if our children are to reach their full potential.

GPA and test scores are important. Students cannot squeak by academically, depending on their athletic talent to carry them through. Both must be a top priority.

Unfortunately, academics often rank a (very distant) second in a student athlete's priorities. For many successful athletes, school is just a hoop to jump through so that they can play. But in these cases, the parent must remind that student that he or she is, first and foremost, a *student*. Parents must do whatever it takes to keep their athletes from being so consumed with their sport that they lose sight of the bigger picture.

This is a lesson I had to teach to Jay, and it was definitely not easy!

By the time he was in high school, Jay was so consumed with being a jock that he let his grades go from the honor roll to barely passing. And in my house, this was not an option. He lost nearly all of his privileges, and I didn't allow him to attend one dance or extra activity until he improved his grades.

I was highly criticized by other parents for being too hard on him, but that did not matter to me as much as making sure Jay kept a healthy balance. Football was not more important than schoolwork. And if I had not gotten his attention as a freshman, he may not have been eligible for the scholarship offers he received as a junior. But thankfully, Jay got the message. He kept his grades up all through high school and college, and I later heard him tell his younger brother how important it was for him to keep his grades up, too.

Parents need to keep track of how their student is doing in school. In this age of technology we can email, call, check homework hotlines or even make an old fashioned trip to the school to find out how our athletes are performing. And it is vital that we do so—regularly! When parents don't pay attention to how their children are doing in school, there can be serious repercussions. Their athletes can find themselves eligible to play, but missing out on the requirements needed to get into the college of their choice.

It happens all the time. And it is a massive waste of potential.

For example, a few years ago, I attended a football combine where a young man ran a 4.2 forty yard dash. The judges made him run it again to make sure they had timed him correctly. The second time he was just as quick. I asked his sister which colleges were recruiting him. To my surprise—no one was! Sadly, I later learned that the young man's 2.1 GPA and low ACT score meant he did not qualify academically for any Division I school. That young man spent a lot of time nurturing his athletic talent, but in the end, his lack of balance hurt him tremendously.

Our children must focus on their academic development. Certainly, a good education will enable them to succeed in any arena of life. But also, academic excellence is *expected* of student athletes. I talk to a lot of college recruiters, and they are very clear on this point. There are too many talented athletes out there to waste time on a child who is not academically eligible to get into their university. In fact, I had one recruiter tell me that he always starts a recruiting visit in the guidance office to check out a prospect's grades. If the grades aren't right, he doesn't bother even to meet the athlete.

Talent cannot be a higher priority than a good education. There are no guarantees that an athlete will be healthy enough to play at the college level, but as long as an athlete has prepared himself to compete academically, his future will always be bright.

Getting Under the Skin

Talent and education will go a long way to helping your student reach his or her full potential. But athletic talent and academic performance are both primarily about who we are on the outside. Focusing only on those two areas means our students spend all their time creating an image, a reputation, a persona for others to see.

The problem, however, is that we must also be concerned with who our students are on the inside. Which brings us to the third area that sports parents need to focus on: *character*. We need to be as concerned about the person our child actually is as we are about what they can do, both on and off the field.

Basically, *character* is who we are in the deepest part of our being. It's "who we are in the dark," as the saying goes. John Wooden once said, "Be more concerned with your character than your reputation because your character is what you really are, while your reputation is merely what others think you are."[2]

Helping our students discover and develop their character is vitally important primarily because our character is what determines how and why we make the choices we do. Let me repeat that: *our character will always determine our choices*. No matter how much potential we have, it is our character that determines the true measure of our success.

81

I was absolutely committed to seeing my sons develop good character. But it was not a guarantee. In Jay's life, for example, his natural athletic skill provided many amazing opportunities, but it also presented potential pitfalls that I was concerned would negatively impact the man he would become.

That's why I prayed regularly for Jay. I prayed that he would stay grounded, that his reputation as a standout football player would not give him a big head. I also spoke with Jay often about who he was becoming. I reminded him that his dream wasn't about him alone. I encouraged him to mentor younger players and remember that God wanted him to use his dream, not just to bless himself, but so that God could bless others through him. In other words, I did all I could to guide him towards the character I wanted him to have.

As a parent, that is our job. And it is not an easy one, by any means. Shepherding Jay towards good character was a constant focus. It took time and energy and lots of prayer, but I was committed to it because the payoff is huge.

We must be committed to seeing our children develop good character. I knew that only character would give Jay the moorings he would need even when I wasn't there. It was vital to his achieving true success. And the same is true for every athlete. Character will enable a good athlete to succeed beyond all expectations.

Archie Griffin is a perfect example.

Griffin is more than talented. He is the only two-time Heisman Trophy winner, won the Big Ten Championship all four years that he played for Ohio State, and then played for seven years in the NFL. But Griffin also focused on his education. After leaving the NFL, he earned an MBA at The Ohio State University and is now the President of OSU's Alumni Association.[3]

However, what is most impressive about Archie Griffin is the character and integrity he displays. Woody Hayes once said he was "a better young man than a football player—and he's the best football player I've ever seen."[4] Griffin has represented Ohio State well for thirty years. He has contributed to many charities, and he is humble and pleasant whenever you meet him. Clearly, this is the kind of character that we want our students to develop.

Unfortunately, for every Archie Griffin, there are hundreds of athletes who display a lack of character. Instead of integrity, they act with immaturity and entitlement. And not surprisingly, this lack of character results in very bad choices. No matter how much talent an athlete has, a lack of character will lead to cracks and breakdowns eventually.

I have seen this happen repeatedly to highly-talented athletes. They are stars in their sports, earning Division I scholarships and, it seems, a clear path to great success. And then everything falls apart. They do something stupid, make a poor decision, get mixed up in things they should have avoided, and it costs them everything. I could easily name player after player whose failures were splashed across the news and whose futures were totally and irrevocably damaged. All because of bad choices. All for lack of character.

Sadly, in some of these cases, it was not just the athletes who suffered. I have seen parents lose their financial stability and even their businesses trying to cover the costs of their athletes' mistakes. In other cases, the athlete's indiscretions resulted in penalties and investigations for their schools and coaches. For these athletes, a choice that seemed like "no big deal" at the time caused damage that they never imagined.

My mother was constantly reminding my boys of this principle. For years, she would call or write my sons every time she saw an athlete make a bad decision, reminding them that they would have to bury her if they did something like that. Finally, Jay called me and said, "Does Grandma think I'm stupid?" I told him, "No, but she wants to make sure you don't **do** something stupid, ruin your future and embarrass the family." Thanks to my mother, my boys had a constant reminder that the decisions they made mattered, and not just for them!

Now, I do realize that these decisions are often out of a parent's control. But they are never out of the student's control. And that is why we must focus on developing character in our athletes as early as possible. Talk about character. Ask them why they are making the choices they're making and how those choices might affect their future and those around them. Encourage them to think about possible consequences. Teach them to ask themselves, "Is this the wise thing to do?"[5] No matter how difficult it is, if a student develops the habit of thinking this way, it will ensure her success in the long run.

Besides all of that, however, good character has become an expected quality for athletes. Regardless of the sport in question, coaches and team leaders are looking for young men and women who demonstrate true character.

The day before the 2007 NFL Draft, *USAToday* ran this headline: "New NFL Policy has teams trying to avoid 'Bad

Apples.'" The article highlighted certain players who would have been top draft choices but whose popularity had steeply declined because of character issues, including legal trouble, substance abuse, and concerns about their coachability. For these young men, poor choices impacted when or if they would be drafted at all.[6]

And even below the professional levels, character is a big deal. Colleges are tired of recruiting talented athletes only to have them become ineligible or un-coachable due to questionable character. They now do background checks and monitor the athlete's social media presence to get a better picture of the person being recruited. They talk with teachers, coaches, and other players. They want to know the whole person, not just the athlete.

A fantastic example of this attitude is Concord University's men's soccer program. Head coach Steve Barrett restarted the program in 2008, and having men on his team who display excellence on the field and in their character is an absolute necessity. When describing his 2012 recruiting class, Coach Barrett commented:

We're really excited with our incoming class, specifically with the quality of play on the field and the character they demonstrate off the field and in the classroom. This class is going to put down a tremendous foundation for the Concord Men's Soccer Program for years to come.

Even in his published descriptions of the individual recruits, Coach Barrett mentions each player's character nearly as often as he does his on-field strengths. Clearly, character is a high priority for this program.[7]

Another example of the recent focus on character is the NAIA, the National Association of Intercollegiate Athletics. The NAIA has 300 member schools which sponsor thirteen different programs including football, baseball, basketball, soccer, swimming, and tennis. But they do not focus entirely on sports. In 2000, they launched an initiative called *Champions of Character* which promotes five key areas of character and provides opportunities for parental involvement and coaches' training. They are committed to developing character in their athletes, at both the high school and college levels.[8]

Our family experienced this same attitude when Jay was being recruited by Ohio State. When then-head coach Jim Tressel visited our home, he spent almost three hours with our family and never once tried to sell us on Ohio State football. He wanted to get to know us, and he shared stories about himself and his family. He made it very clear that he recruited families and that he was looking for players with integrity.

Talent alone will never be enough for our children to achieve their full potential. They must have a broader focus. Instead of concentrating only on being eligible, we need to help our students develop their athletic talent, make sure they are prepared academically, and train them to value their character as highly as their athletic achievements.

Making it Happen

Of course, all of that sounds great. Who wouldn't like to see their children achieve that kind of balance in their lives? But simply wishing for it isn't going to make it happen. We have to do something about it. So how can we, as parents, actually help our children develop their talent, their education and their character all at the same time?

Obviously, it won't be easy.

Some parents focus too much on the future. They concentrate on graduation, the Olympics, the championship game, or the next season, and they miss the daily process of their student's growth. These parents forget that parenting is like building a Lego house. An individual piece may seem insignificant. But when all the pieces have been put together, an amazing creation results. The same is true for children. Individual moments can seem mundane. But each of those moments works together to create the end result, the person that child will become. Focusing too much on the future means we miss *today*, where our student's actual growth is happening right before our eyes.

On the other hand, many more parents focus too much on the past. They moan about the mistakes they've already made, the opportunities they've already missed, and they figure they can't make it work now. But that is also the wrong attitude to take.

Certainly, we don't want to look back over our lives and lament over what should have been and what we could have done as parents. But focusing backwards will not get us going in the right direction, either. As my good friend always says: "We gotta "stop 'should-ing' and 'could-ing' all over the place and start doing." Her point is simple. Stop looking back at what's been done and starting doing *now* what you need to do to move forward. You can't change the past, so let it go and start focusing on today—where you still have lots of opportunities to create the success you long to see.

We will best enable our students to find a good balance in life by focusing on where they are right now. As parents, we need to be looking for opportunities every day to teach our children how to develop each of the three key areas of life. The Bible describes it this way: *And ye shall teach them to your children, speaking of them when thou sittest in thine house, and when thou walkest by the way, when thou liest down, and when thou risest up (Deut. 11:19).* In other words, parenting is a lifestyle, rather than series of lessons.

Whatever you want your children to really understand needs to be woven through every part of their life, every part of their day. You can't just chat about it during the "big" moments. You need to ask them about how today's practice went. Let them know that you care whether they got today's homework done and why. Talk to them about the choices they're facing right now. Be willing to be part of their whole lives.

But simply talking to them will never be enough. Talking more (or louder) is not going to help them achieve balance. It probably won't accomplish anything at all! Instead, we have to do our best to *model* balance for them.

You are your child's first teacher, coach and mentor. Countless studies have concluded that parents have the greatest influence on their children—more than friends, more than social media, more than anything. In other words, you are the pattern your athlete is using to mold his life. You may not be helping her develop a specific swim stroke or practice a particular play, but you are teaching her, every day, simply by how you are living life in front of her.

As parents, we must ask ourselves, "What kind of balance am I modeling for my children?" And we must be honest in our assessment because displaying a healthy balance is not easy.

Many well-intentioned parents spend thousands of dollars to buy their children the best of everything: designer clothes, the best games, and an overabundance of electronics. They work eighty hours a week, or two jobs, trying to buy things that their children don't really appreciate, and they miss seeing their children in action on the field, court or diamond. These parents are modeling an unbalanced life.

But even if we aren't buying our children every new gadget and toy, we still may not be displaying balance. We can focus so much on our family's image or reputation that we miss giving our children what is really important—time, memories, and solid values. We care more about what others think of us than about what our children see in us. And that, too, is imbalance. Yes, we should want to look presentable to others, and we should put time and effort into taking care of ourselves and our things, but emphasizing what's on the outside, without also prioritizing character, is a sure way to set our children up for failure.

Modeling good balance is difficult. In fact, it's impossible. The truth is, we will mess up. None of us is always balanced. So it's okay to let your children see you struggle in this area. Don't pretend to be perfect. Our students need role models, not supermodels! Let them see when you do it right, and talk them through the times when you do it poorly. They will appreciate your honesty, and they will learn to handle both successes and failures. And that is what being a model is all about.

Seeing your child earn a scholarship to a quality program means rearing a son or daughter who is focused on character, good values and integrity. This kind of success is not bought, it is taught—and the one who can teach it most effectively is you. And modeling is the key.

The Big Picture

So where does all this leave us?

Being eligible is important, but it not the highest priority. If we focus only on our children's talent, we will miss the bigger picture that is vital to our students' success in every area of life, not just sports. We must help our students find and maintain a balanced focus so that they mature into well-rounded people, not merely accomplished athletes.

Helping your student find a balance between talent, education and character is the hallmark of successful parenting. It is not an overnight pursuit. It requires patience, hard work, and humility. But seeing your sons and daughters mature into capable and independent adults is worth all of the effort it takes.

Endnotes

[1]Myles Munroe, *Understanding Your Potential* (Shippensdale, PA: Destiny Image, 1991): n.pag. 12 Oct. 2012 <http://books.google.com/books?id=TOyrYvHXoBYC&pg=PP10&lpg=PP1&ots=Th6hkLkOQR&dq=understanding+your+potential>

[2]ESPN.com staff, "The Wizard's Wisdom - Woodenisms," 2012, ESPN, 4 June 2010. 13 Oct. 2012 <http://sports.espn.go.com/ncb/news/story?id=5249709>

[3]"Archie Griffin," Wikipedia: The Free Encyclopedia, 5 Sept. 2012, Wikimedia. 13 Oct. 2012

<http://en.wikipedia.org/w/index/php?title=Archie_Griffin&oldid=510874770>

[4]Chris Graber, "Griffin Honored with $2 Million Donation," The Lantern, 13 Jan. 2010. 13 Oct. 2012 <http://www.thelantern.com/campus/griffin-honored-with-2-million-donation-1.1010903#.UHlXLrQlYlJ>

[5]Andy Stanley, The Best Question Ever (New York: Random House Digital, 2004): n. pag. 13 Oct. 2012. <http://books.google.com/books?id=FZPKloLaSMwC&printsec=frontcover#v=onepage&q&f=false>

[6]Tom Weir, "New NFL Policy Has Teams Trying to Avoid 'Bad Apple,'" 19 Apr. 2007, USA Today. 13 Oct. 2012 <http://usatoday30.usatoday.com/sports/football/draft/2007-04-19-conduct-cover_N.htm>

Chapter Five
Creating a Dream Team

"There is no such thing as a self-made man. You will reach your goals only with the help of others." George Shinn (former owner of New Orleans Hornets)

A Dream Team

In 1992, sports fans enjoyed one of the greatest athletic experiences of all time. That year, professional basketball players were first allowed to compete in the Olympics, and Team USA overflowed with talent. They were called the Dream Team, a group of basketball legends including Michael Jordan, Larry Bird, Karl Malone, and Patrick Ewing, among others. Even the coaches were the best of the best. And of course, they won the gold without so much as a challenge from any opponent they faced.

Most people were convinced (and still are) that the Dream Team was the greatest sports team ever assembled.[1]

And no wonder. Our culture worships "superstar" athletes. We celebrate the Michael Jordans, the athletes who excel at their chosen sports, the seemingly unbeatable players who bring wins with them wherever they go.

But while there may be star athletes, there is really no such thing as a stand-alone athlete. In 1992, none of those immensely talented players could have won gold on their own. They needed each other. Even the best of the best needed a committed and unified support system to get to the top.

And the same is true for your athlete.

In order for your child to achieve his dreams, he needs a team of people who will support and assist him along the way. A star quarterback needs a player to catch his perfect pass. The star forward cannot dunk unless a teammate passes him the ball. Even in individual sports, athletes depend on their coaches and trainers. Yes, they have to play the sport (and play it very well), but they need a team of people around them to make them truly successful.

Thankfully, most sports parents know this. We work hard to make sure that our students have the support they need: the right team, the best coach, all the necessary resources. We spare no expense to provide the best network possible. We understand that, in order for our athletes to reach their goals, they must be surrounded with the right people.

They need their very own "Dream Team."

Making the Team
But what many sports parents don't realize is that we, too, need a stellar support system.

We pour time and money into creating the perfect network for our athletes, but we neglect our own support needs. Parents, this cannot be. I am convinced that every sports parent needs a Dream Team, too, a group of committed people who can assist him or her in exactly the same way that our athletes' teammates and coaches support them.

Members of your Dream Team will provide vital support for your student. They can be friends and mentors whenever she needs them. Team members can offer a ride to and from practice or be another cheering fan in the stands. Your Dream Team will love on, defend and challenge your student in ways that you alone will never be able to do.

But even more, a Dream Team benefits you as a parent. There will always be someone ready to drive your child home from a game or to offer him an open door until you get home from work. Having a Dream Team lets you provide comfort and safety for your child, even when you cannot be there. And these friends are also mentors for you, providing feedback and advice as you navigate the difficult world of sports parenting.

And yet, despite all these benefits, parents rarely take the time to build such a network for themselves and for their families.

There are lots of excuses. It is difficult to find good people you can depend on. You don't have time to connect with people this way. You don't know how to ask someone to join your team. And...all of those things are true. Building a Dream Team requires time and energy and attention. It isn't always easy. Sometimes it can seem downright impossible.

But it is, I assure you, worth every ounce of effort.

My Personal Dream Team

The idea that parents should create a personal Dream Team is not a new one. We hear it regularly from parenting experts and child psychologists. It's even the basis of the familiar proverb: "It takes a village to raise a child." From every direction, we are reminded that we cannot adequately manage the job of parenting our children on our own, that we have to build a support system for ourselves and our families.

But I learned the value of this network first (and most powerfully) from my mother.

My mom always said, "You can't make it in this world by yourself." And she would know. She was divorced when I was seven years old and worked swing shifts at the local hospital. Because she was not always able to be home when we were, she developed a network of people who could help my siblings and me with any concern or issue we encountered. These authority figures and role models were vital for our family's survival, and by creating this support network, my mother provided for me a valuable parenting model.

As it turned out, I needed that model immensely after I, too, became a mom. Like my mom's, my life has not been a smooth one. Like any parent, I have faced many unexpected twists and turns. When my boys were very young, I had a job that required a lot of travel, and I had to find ways to provide for them when I could not be home. Even more significantly, I was married, divorced, and remarried while my boys were growing up.

In other words, doing it "on my own" was simply not an option.

Instead, I relied on the example my mother had provided, and I began to develop a group of people, an inner circle, whom I could trust to help me during my sons' formative years. They watched my boys for me, picked them up from school, helped them with homework, and took them to practices. They stepped in and helped when I had to be gone, so that my sons' lives were disrupted as little as possible. These friends, neighbors and family members kept my family's dreams alive, and I don't know where I or my children would have ended up without the love and support of these wonderful people.

In the world of sports parenting, it really does "take a village to raise a child."

We must create a support system, no matter how difficult it might seem. As parents, especially as sports parents, we must recognize that we are going to need assistance to raise our children successfully, both as athletes and as human beings. And your best resource will always be your Dream Team, that select group of friends and mentors who are ready to lend a hand whenever you need it.

Creating the Team

So, are you ready to put together a Dream Team for your family? Good. But what's the first step? Whom should you include? What types of people make good team members for your family?

There are two important qualities you need to consider.

First of all, you must take *attitude* into account. Attitude will always affect what a person will accomplish. A student who never comes to practice isn't going to stay on the football team very long. The player who doesn't give 100% will not get very much playing time. In sports and in life, no one wants to be on a team with a negative, lazy, or undependable player.

But this principle is particularly important for your Dream Team. Your children will absorb the attitudes they are exposed to, so you need to find people who have positive and motivated attitudes, who see the big picture, and who know how to deal well with difficulty.

One of my grandmother's favorite saying was, "Stick with the people who are doing something!" She encouraged my mom and her siblings to connect with people who were dreaming big and willing to work hard to get there. My mom repeated that saying to me more times than I can count, but more than that, she lived it. The people she exposed us to as role models and authority figures were those people who held themselves to high standards and pushed themselves to do the best they could do in every area of their lives. I have tried to do the same for my children. I wanted them to meet and be influenced by people who would inspire them positively and push them forward, rather than dragging them down or holding them back from being the best athlete and person they could be.

The second quality you need to emphasize is *diversity*.

Your Dream Team should include a variety of positive adult role models. I connected my boys with teachers, business professionals, ministers and others whom I hoped would have a positive influence on their lives. Whenever they expressed an interest in something, I would find someone in that field whom I respected, and I would get advice from them on my sons' behalf or I would make sure they met my boys personally. These adults provided for my boys examples of how wonderful their life could be if they did the right things, worked hard for what they wanted, and exhibited good character.

Another important group of people to include on your Dream Team is your child's coach and his teammates' parents. Other parents can assist you with the logistics of managing games and practices, and they also can be moral support for your student when you cannot be there to watch them play. In the same way, coaches are a vital part of any Dream Team. Let them know that you are interested in your child's success by getting to know them and helping wherever you can. This will go a long way to ensuring your child's success in and out of the sports arena.

Positive role models and other sports figures are obvious choices for a parenting Dream Team. The final segment of the network, however, may surprise you. These team members are some of the most vital, and they will have the most influence on your children, either positively or negatively. I'm speaking of your child's friends.

As protectors and advocates in a child's life, it is important for parents to know their children's friends. I am very serious about this—take the time to get to know your child's friends and their parents. It was not unusual for me to take my teenage boys to their friend's house so that I could introduce myself to their parents. I was even known to come to their friends' cars and give mini-lectures about safe driving or to stop by a party they were attending to see what was going on.

My boys would sometimes be embarrassed by such appearances, but I needed to know who they were spending time with. It was important to me that they were surrounded with people who were building them up and helping them succeed. The same needs to be true for every sports parent. You need to know who your child is spending time with and the potential influence those people will have on your student's life and future.

Clearly, there are other possible team members whom I have not mentioned specifically. If they live close by, family members can be a vital part of your support system. Church members, backyard neighbors, babysitters and many others can also provide your family the support you need. But whomever you include, the key is to start today. Begin as soon as possible to build a team of people who can assist you in the pursuit of your child's success.

You need a Dream Team.

Making the Team Work For You

But having a Dream Team is not enough. You have to actually use them for your team to do your family any good.

Unfortunately, our culture often defines greatness as the ability to succeed without help. We learn to depend on only ourselves, and we feel like a failure if we have to "give in" and ask for assistance. So even if we have a group of people who is willing to help us when needed, we often try to just muddle through without ever taking them up on that offer.

But no more.

A Dream Team is necessary for our survival as sports parents, and we must discipline ourselves to utilize the team in whatever ways we need them. And every family is different; what worked for my boys and me may not be the best system for you. You will have to discover how best to manage your children's needs, but here are three principles that will help you get the most benefit from your support system.

1. **Let Them In.** It is your responsibility to recruit a Dream Team. But even more importantly, you must know what's going on in your child's life so that you know when you need to call in a member of your network for a consultation. See yourself as the bridge connecting your children to each available resource. Know what your child is facing and then put your child in direct contact with someone who can best help them.

In most cases, parents hope they will be the best resource for their children, but that simply may not always be the case. Many teenagers, particularly, find it easier to have conversations about sex, a difficult decision, and their struggles with school, friends, or their sport with someone other than a parent. While you should be open to talking about such things with your student, with a Dream Team in place, you will already have others in their lives whom they can talk to and whom you trust to talk to them. I will always be grateful for my dear friends who pulled my boys aside and reinforced lessons I was trying to teach them.

But remember that a Dream Team supports both the athlete *and* the parent. Not only could I rely on team members to counsel my sons, I could ask these same friends for advice when dealing with a difficult decision or situation. They would also pull me aside when they thought that I was using the wrong approach with my boys or that I was somehow getting off course. And while I might not have always agreed with their concerns, having their input helped me to evaluate my own parenting decisions more effectively.

The more I was willing to rely on my Dream Team, and the more they proved themselves a valuable asset in my parenting arsenal, the easier it was to let them assist me. It takes practice and a little bit of humility to use your Dream Team well, but developing that habit will mean you always have the help you need, when you or your child need it.

2. **Choose Wisely.** It is vital that you only include people on your Dream Team who have proven themselves positive and beneficial friends and mentors. Not everyone is able to provide the support you need, so do not feel obligated to accept just anyone into your inner circle.

This principle is particularly true in regard to your student's friends. Whenever my boys brought home someone whose behavior I didn't like, I would talk to the friend and tell them what I did not approve of. I expected all of my sons' friends to follow our house rules and to respect me and our home while they were in it. If a particular friend was not inclined to submit to my rules, then he was no longer welcome in our home.

And while it is not always immediately clear what sort of influence a friend will have, you need to trust your instincts. If something in my spirit told me that a particular child was not a good influence, I would firmly tell my son that he should find someone else to hang out with. I did not require that step very often, but every time it happened, my boys found out that it was a good decision. One young man, in particular, had never done anything specific to upset me; I just knew there was something about him I didn't like. I asked my son to stop hanging out with him, and we later found out that the young man was dealing drugs. He was definitely not the kind of influence I wanted my sons to have!

Whether friends or adults, you need to make sure that you choose wisely those people you allow into your inner circle. Be careful in your selection process, and if you find out later that someone is not the influence you had hoped, do not be afraid to remove them from the Team. Getting the right people into place may take some work, and you may even make some mistakes along the way. But with a little work, you will soon have an all-star roster of people who will be able to help you achieve all that you set out to do.

3. **Be Flexible**. Your team can and must change. The 1992 Dream Team would no longer be able to compete at the Olympic level; instead, a new group of athletes will work every four years to earn that title (and another U.S. gold). The same is true for your Dream Team. A good team

must be flexible; it needs to change with the current circumstances.

Your Team may need to change because your child has changed. As your child grows and matures, she will need new and different support. Someone who was a great influence when she was nine may no longer provide the same benefit when she is sixteen. One coach may have been perfect through the lower levels of a sport, but your son may need a new coach to move into the highest levels of competition. You need to be flexible and know that the Team you originally put together may not always be the right one for right now.

On occasion, the Team may need to change because a Team Member no longer fits. Some friends and families are part of your life only for a season, and then it's time to move on. It may not be a conscious decision, as much as two families simply drifting away, but if a friendship is dissolving, sometimes it is necessary to simply let it go and see what new opportunities open up in the current stage of your family's life.

Most importantly, don't be afraid to disassociate with a person who no longer has your child's best interest at heart. You may have shared the same parenting philosophy with another parent for years, but if they begin to allow their children new autonomy that you know is not okay for your child, you need to remove that parent from your Dream Team.

Learning to utilize your Dream Team is vital. Connect your student to the people who can best help them. Pay attention to the influence that Team members, especially friends, are having on your athlete. And be flexible. Applying these principles will ensure that your family has the support you need to pursue your dream wholeheartedly.

Working Together—Everyone Wins

I once read a parable that illustrates the Dream Team concept perfectly:

"There was a Saint who had a vision about what it was like in Hell & Heaven.

In Hell he saw a huge table laden with food in the center. Surrounding the table were starving people who all had very long forks attached to the ends of their arms. They could stab the food, but the forks were too long for them to put the food in their mouths. They were all screaming in frustration as they tried to eat the food that they longed for.

In Heaven, the saint saw the exact same table laden with food and people with the long forks at the ends of their arms. However, here the people were all smiling and enjoying the food. What they were doing was stabbing the food and putting it in *each other's* mouths!"

Whether we are talking about your daughter's volleyball team, the Olympic men's basketball team, or your personal Dream Team, we must realize that we cannot succeed on our own. Only by working together will we be able to survive and thrive through all the changes and. circumstances that life will throw at us.

The path to victory, in sports and in parenting, is all about learning to work together. And the most important way that you, as a sports parent, can do that is by creating and using a Dream Team that can help your family's dreams come true.

Endnotes

[1]"This Day in Sports: The Dream Team Takes Gold in Barcelona." 8 Aug. 2010, ESPN, 2012. 14 Oct. 2012 <http://espn.go.com/blog/sportscenter/post/_/id/71610/this-day-in-sports-the-dream-team-takes-gold-in-barcelona>

Chapter Six
Turn Your Volume Down and Your Ear Up!

"The most basic of all human needs is the need to understand and be understood. The best way to understand people is to listen to them." Ralph Nichols

Communication Issues

I have a problem. It's kind of hard to admit...but I talk a lot.

Of course, anyone who knows me is probably laughing as they read this. Because the truth is, I talk A LOT! I can talk to strangers without a problem. Put me in a room with good friends, and we'll chat for hours. I even talk in my sleep!

Not that talking is a bad thing. God has blessed me greatly through the use of my mouth, both to make a living and to help people (like you!). But there is also a downside to being a talkative person. I speak so much that I sometimes forget to listen to what everyone around me is saying.

Thankfully, I know I'm not the only one. We all wrestle with our mouths in some way. Some of us talk too much. Others talk too little. But no matter our particular issue, we all understand that communication is important. To succeed at anything, we must learn to communicate well. It's necessary for our student athletes. And as sports parents, it's even more important for us.

Communication 101
So while I promise not to bore you with complex theories about good communication, I do need to cover a few basic ideas.

Obviously, nothing I'm about to say is difficult. Good communication is, actually, quite simple. But simple and easy are not the same thing. It's easy to understand what to do. Doing it well, on the other hand, is often much more complicated than it might at first seem.

With that in mind, then, let me quickly cover two basic principles for good communication.

First, we must learn to *listen well*. My son's friend Matt often says, "Turn your volume down and your ear up!" In other words, a good listener chooses to talk less and listen more. He will restrict his own words and, instead, encourage others to share their ideas and concerns. He puts a higher priority on the other person's input than he does on his own.

Listening well is about respect. It is a clear sign that you respect another person enough to notice what she has to say. Think about it. We only download podcasts from speakers whose ideas we want to hear. And in real life, it's exactly the same. We only stop and listen to the people we consider worthy of our time.

In parenting, the same principle holds true. When we stop and listen to our kids, we let them know that they are valuable. Multitasking while our children are sharing with us sends a clear message that we do not consider them important. As hard as it can sometimes be, we cannot just mumble "uh-huh" occasionally while we read or check email; we must choose to listen. Our children need to know that we think them worthwhile. They want to be so important to us that we stop what we are doing, look them in the eye, and hear what they have to say. So that's what we need to do.

Listening to your children is also about relationship building. When we listen, we can learn from and about our children. While most parents think they really *know* their kids, inside and out, our perceptions are often completely off the mark, especially if we've never let our children share with us who they really are. Listening allows us to learn who they are and what they want out of life.

If you can, learn to listen to your children while they are young. A young child who discovers that his parents really care to hear what he has to say will continue to talk to his parents as he grows. But it is also never too late to start. Many rocky relationships between parents and teens would be transformed if parents would choose to listen. Let your children share honestly, even if it's difficult for you to hear, and you will be surprised how opportunities open for you to give advice and assistance, even to a child who has never wanted your input before. That is the power of listening well.

So the first principle of good communication is listening well: taking the time to let our children talk to us and really hearing what they have to say. And the second, equally important principle is similar. I call it "listening with our eyes, not just our ears." In other words, we need to be *paying attention.*

The vast majority of all communication happens without any words at all. So as parents, we need to be actively paying attention to our children: how they behave, how they react, when they stop talking (and why). We need to hear what they are saying when they aren't using any words at all.

This skill is especially necessary for parents of older children. Teenagers may not always verbalize what they think or feel, but their actions will show us what is really going on. We might recognize that there is a problem by their tone or how they react to a certain situation. Suddenly they stop hanging out with an old friend, or they start hanging out with new ones. They no longer want to go to a favorite park. Their grades suddenly drop or they lose interest in a favorite hobby or their sport of choice. All of these things are signals, attempts by our kids to tell us what's going on inside of them. And we have to be paying attention so we can recognize the messages they may not be able to tell us with words.

Paying attention was a lesson I learned very late in my boys' growing up years. In my case, it happened in Joshua Alexander's tenth grade year when I discovered, out of the blue, that he is an incredible poet. I was in his room looking through some papers when I discovered a notebook full of the most amazing poetry. Inside the front cover of the notebook Josh had written this note, "Well you finally found it, this is part two of a three volume set but the real poetry is inside of me." I was reduced to tears.

It was such an important moment for me as a parent. I realized I had been so caught up with Jay's success and career path that I hadn't taken the time to really get to know all of who Josh was. And he had patiently waited for me. He wasn't hiding anything from me, but until that moment, I didn't have the eyes to see who he had become.

And needless to say, I took the lesson to heart. I started to listen with my eyes and well as my ears. I began to talk to my boys, all of them, and to pay closer attention to how they spent their time and what they liked and didn't like. And because of those changes, I have learned so much (and continue to learn much) about my children. As a result, I have developed much more genuine connections with my boys and was able to support them each in more effective ways.

Good communication is always about connecting with people. As a parent, you need to work hard to understand your children, not just at the surface, but deep inside. You need to know why they love to swim or what drives them to be the best football player they can be. And if you are persistent, they are usually willing to share these parts of themselves with you.

Learning to understand my boys did not come easily to me, but I realized that if I truly wanted to know what was going on in my children's life, that was exactly what I needed to pursue. I needed to talk less and listen more. I needed to pay closer attention. I needed to offer them an open and willing ear and then let them share with me who they were discovering themselves to be.

It is not an easy process, I assure you. But the relationship you will develop with your children as you learn to communicate with them well will be more than worth the effort.

A Whole New Ballgame
All parents need to listen well and pay attention. But for sports parents, good communication is especially vital.

In order to effectively advocate for your child, you have to know your student. You have to be listening to what your student is saying about school, her sport, his friends, everything, as well as paying attention to what he or she is not saying about all of those areas. Only by knowing your student well can you make good decisions, decisions that will actually benefit him or her, both today and in the future.

But communicating *with* your student is not enough. As an advocate, you will also be called on to communicate *for* your athlete. You will be the primary voice for your athlete, at least until they are older. You will need to communicate with coaches, other parents, officials, the media, and others.

That is why you must learn to communicate well.

Whether or not a sports parent can communicate well has the potential to affect her athlete. During the 2012 Olympic Games, the media had a field day when swimmer Ryan Lochte's mother described his dating life as having lots of one-night stands. What she meant, she later clarified, was that he goes on a lot of first dates, but doesn't like to lead girls on.[1] But, her lack of experience communicating in the public eye lead to much criticism and gossip about both Ryan and his mom. What you say can affect your child and his or her career or reputation, so you must be careful with your words at all times.

Also, how you communicate will be the model for how your son or daughter communicates, too. If you yell, so will he. If you gossip about other players, so will she. If you are disrespectful to officials and coaches, your athlete will develop that habit as well. You are the model, the foundation on which your child will build his or her communication skills, so it is vital that you learn to do it well.

Every sports parent wants to be prepared for the variety of communication situations he or she may face. So let's look briefly at how best to respond to the most common opportunities that can arise while you are advocating for your child.

Communicating with Coaches

Interacting with coaches will be the most common situation that you will face. As I mentioned in Chapter 2, your child's coach must always be addressed with respect and listened to attentively. When he or she makes a decision you disagree with, you must respond calmly, without yelling or losing your cool. When asking for feedback or clarification, make sure that your words and tone are not accusatory, but kind and supportive. Whatever you do, communicate to your child's coach that you support him or her and want to help the team succeed in any way you can.

Communicating with other Parents or Athletes

Thankfully, most of the communication you will have with other parents or athletes will be, by nature, positive. But be intentional about how to you speak to other parents. Make sure that you are friendly and helpful, as much as possible, especially to the parents of athletes who are new to the team. And obviously, opposing players and their families should be treated kindly. Yes, you want your child or her team to defeat their squad, but keep your words and manner courteous and positive—before, during and after the game.

Communicating with Officials or the Media

As a sports parent, you will often find yourself communicating with people in official positions outside your team or school. These officials will usually be referees or judges, but they may also be recruiters, college officials, and the media. You must be very, very careful about what you say and how you say it in any situation involving someone in an official capacity.

Refs may not always make good calls, but they should be treated with respect, no matter how obviously your son just got fouled. College recruiters and school officials need to be dealt with honestly, but respectfully, as well. White lies, parental bravado, and over-the-top demands have no place in an interview or recruiting visit. Being genuine and respectful, truthful and fair will do more for your child's chances than any amount of falsity. And whenever you find yourself dealing with the media, think carefully about what you want to say before you offer the response they have asked for. Answer their questions as honestly as you can, but don't be afraid to decline comment. Especially with the media, it is better to remain silent than to see your words go viral in a negative way.

Walking in their Shoes

There is one final area of communication that must be addressed. In our high-tech world, perfecting your basic listening skills is not enough. Sports parents must also master the realities of online communication and the use of social media.

When we were growing up, our parents knew what we were thinking or doing because they overheard us on the phone with our friends. But today, our children text instead of talk. They don't blast their stereos; they are perpetually attached to their ear buds. They spend hours connecting on Facebook, Twitter and YouTube or playing video games.

And none of that, by itself, is a problem.

In fact, many of us use this form of communication every day. We make calls, send text messages or email, or read Facebook and Twitter. We recognize that online communication is helpful, even powerful. But for our children, the use of social media is fundamentally essential to their lives, and if we don't grasp this fact, we will miss out on an important segment of our students' interactions.

We must become fluent in the realm of social media. To ignore the influence of social media means that we risk losing a significant amount of influence in our children's lives. That does not mean you should be a Facebook junkie or become an expert at sending texts! Your goal should not be to become your child's best online buddy. But you do need to be familiar with and capable of using the technology and social media options that your student is participating in because, unless we find ways to bridge the communication gap, they will consider us totally irrelevant. We will be tuned out by a generation of young people who consider these media the primary mechanism for communicating and connecting with the world around them.

Whether you like it or not, parenting your athlete's social networking is a necessary reality in our digital world. You need to know what your child is posting and reading on Facebook, Google+, Pinterest, and Twitter, and you need to be aware of who is connecting with your students, too. Periodically ask your child to show you their Twitter or Facebook accounts. Respect their privacy, but set limits on how and when they use these sites.

We must teach our students what effective communication is, both mediated and face-to-face. They need to know that using social media is perfectly acceptable, but only if they do it well. Make sure they know that you care about how they use these sites, as well as the inherent dangers the online world presents. Encourage your athletes to use wisdom and discretion in these arenas because the repercussions of poor media usage can be devastating.

Nearly every week we hear of athletes who learned this lesson the hard way. During the 2012 Olympics, for example, a Greek runner was dropped from her country's team for a tweet she posted making a racist remark.[2] And members of the American team also came under fire for personal comments they posted on Twitter.[3] But even for non-Olympic athletes, poor use of social media can be disastrous.

Many colleges now look at these sites to determine how the students they are recruiting are portrayed. In 2007, *USAToday* ran an article highlighting these concerns and offering multiple examples of student-athletes being sanctioned for posting online pictures or comments that were in poor taste or put their program in a bad light. In one instance, some (underage) athletes were suspended for posting a picture of themselves holding liquor bottles and cash. But other examples were also included:

> Two LSU swimmers were removed from the team after making disparaging comments about their coaches on Facebook, and a Colorado football player and cross country runner were issued harassment tickets by campus police after sending a racially threatening Facebook message to a Hispanic cross country runner.[4]

Clearly, our children must recognize that what they post matters! In the moment, most posts or tweets will seem innocent. But these online postings can and do can have a huge impact on whether or not a student is eligible for athletic competition or scholarships. Even more important, what our students post online can affect their reputations and their character. The repercussions of poor media usage can last forever, long after the athlete has stopped playing his sport. Encourage your student to think about how they communicate online and whether their online lives are going to help or hurt their chances in their sport and in life.

Missing the Message
Still, even with the best of intentions and all the advice in the world, miscommunication happens. A phone call gets missed. An email is misunderstood. A newspaper misquotes your comments about the coach. Unfortunately, this sort of thing is going to occur.

So what can you do when communication breaks down? What can you do when misunderstanding or lack of clear communication interferes with your family or your athlete's goals?

You apologize, learn from the mistake, and start again.

At the end of Joshua Alexander's sophomore year, he began to complain of his leg hurting. Now, Joshua tended to be slightly dramatic, so I told him to "suck it up" and put some ice on it. He would come in several times a week going on and on about how his leg hurt at practice. I told him that was part of playing sports and he should mention it to his trainer. I still felt he was being overly dramatic and didn't want to start coddling him unnecessarily.

Finally, though, after an entire month, I realized that I needed to have it checked out. I felt so bad when his doctor reported that he had pulled his hamstring and needed two months of physical therapy! Clearly, I did not qualify for mom of the year awards for that one!

But I did learn an important lesson.

If I had paid more attention and listened better to my son, I would have realized that something was wrong and gotten help earlier. And when I did realize the extent of Josh's injury, I quickly apologized for not hearing what he was saying. And I learned to take more seriously his complaints, particularly about injuries.

You may not be able to take back what you yelled at the ref or to retract the quotation the newspaper included with your name on it, but you can take responsibility for your mistake, apologize, and then move on. Good communication is never going to be perfect. But small mistakes do not need to cause major problems. With practice and persistence, you and your athlete will learn together how to communicate with each other and with the world around you.

Putting it all Together

If you desire to help your child succeed as a student, citizen and athlete, you must turn your volume down and turn your ear up. You need to respectfully listen to what your athlete is saying and pay attention to what he isn't saying. On a personal level, take the time to really get to know your child, learn what motivates him, get an understanding of where she wants to go, and use this knowledge to develop a game plan to take him or her to the next level. On a public level, learn to communicate well with coaches, officials and others, and make sure that your online communication is as respectful and positive as your verbal communication is.

Good communication is a vital skill for athletes, but it is even more imperative that sports parents take the time to develop their communication skills as well. Modeling positive communication to your students will enable them to achieve the success they long to achieve, on the field and in life.

Endnotes

[1]Nicole Auerbach, "Ryan Lochte's Mom Clears up One-night-stand Talk," 3 Aug. 2012, *USA Today*. 18 Oct. 2012 <http://www.usatoday.com/sports/olympics/london/swimming/story/2012-08-03/ryan-lochte-mom-clears-up-talk-of-one-night-stands/56737510/1>.

[2]Roxanna Scott, "Athlete Ousted from Olympics for Twitter Comment," 25 July 2012, *USA Today*. 18 Oct. 2012. <http://www.usatoday.com/sports/olympics/london/story/2012-07-25/Athlete-booted-from-Games-for-tweet/56478062/1>.

[3]John D. Sutter, "Welcome to the Twitter Olympics," 1 Aug. 2012, *CNN*. 18 Oct. 2012

<http://www.cnn.com/2012/08/01/tech/social-media/welcome-twitter-olympics/index.html>.

[4]Kyle Oppenhuizen, "Schools Creating New Rules for Social Networking Policies," 28 July 2008, *USA Today*. 18 Oct. 2012 <http://www.usatoday.com/sports/college/2008-07-27-social-networks_N.htm>.

Chapter Seven
Play It Safe

"Obviously we will talk about doing everything we can to make our sport as safe as possible." Troy Vincent

I will never forget the most protective mother I've ever met.

I was on a walk, taking a few minutes to enjoy the world outside my door, and passed a flock of Canadian geese. There were lots of fuzzy little goslings to watch, and I was laughing at their baby antics and not paying attention to exactly how close I was getting to the group.

That's when she charged me.

Apparently concerned for the health and well-being of her little brood, this mother goose rushed at me, flapping her wings and hissing. I was so startled that I took off running, which was certainly a sight to see because I am

NOT a runner. But I was not about to face the wrath of that excited female, so I escaped as quickly as I could.

Looking back, it was quite a funny moment. And needless to say, I learned a valuable lesson about getting too close to animal babies. But it also started me thinking about a parent's innate desire to protect her children.

Think about all we do to safeguard our students. We make sure they are dressed appropriately; we try to provide nutritious meals so that they can grow. We monitor their activity to make sure they have balance in their lives and keep a watchful eye on who they are interacting with. Every day, we check the news for possible threats to safety.

Clearly, a parent's instinct to protect is not an attitude that needs to be taught. Once that little baby is put into your arms, you are ready to shield her from anything. I know this was true in my life. There was nothing I would not do to keep my boys safe. I was always ready to defend and protect them, no matter what.

But as natural as it is for parents to protect their children, for sports parents, the focus is even more necessary. As we watch and advocate for our students, their safety has to be an absolute priority. Certainly coaches, trainers, and schools help create an environment of safe participation. But sports parents also bear significant responsibility in this area. More than anyone else, it is the parents who must maintain a consistent focus on their athletes' health and well-being.

On the other hand, we must also recognize that competing in athletics does involve risk. Injuries happen. The emotional ups and downs of sports can be difficult for some children to navigate. Thankfully, most sports parents understand this reality. We are willing to deal with the potential harms because of the benefits that sports offer, too. But even as we search for the balance between acknowledging the risks and encouraging their participation, we cannot neglect our athletes' safety.

And that is sometimes easier said than done.

Despite our best intentions, our emphasis on safety can easily moderate. We have to wear many hats, juggle many priorities, all while trying to keep a careful watch on our children—and sometimes, we get distracted. We want to protect our athletes. We want to make sure they are safe. But with so much on our plates, we sometimes lose focus.

Oddly enough, it was some more geese that brought this lesson home for me. I was on another walk, passing by a large flock, but this time the birds were crowding around a couple who was throwing them bread crumbs. They were so distracted by the crumbs that they were not paying much attention to their babies. I got quite close, but not one goose tried to scare me away.

These geese were not intentionally neglecting their young. But with the right distraction, even the most attentive parent can lose focus, prioritizing something else above his child's safety. As sports parents, we must strive to prevent that from happening. Regardless of what is clamoring for our attention, we need to keep safety a priority.

For the rest of this chapter, then, I want to walk you through some of the most important aspects of sports safety that parents must consider. Evaluate these areas carefully in relationship to your particular situation and athlete. I assure you, your child's well-being could depend on it.

Physical Safety

We will start in the most obvious place—physical safety. Parents should be aware of the potential injuries their student might encounter during training and competition. Of course, a single chapter in a single book is not going to cover all the possible injuries that an athlete can incur. And obviously, most sports injuries are accidents, so there is very little that a parent on the sidelines can do in those cases.

However, there are two significant safety issues that parents can and should be attentive to: nutrition and on-field safety. These are the most common areas of injury or concern, so they are the ones that parents need the most information about. Thankfully, there is plenty of good information available. But it is up to parents (and coaches and athletes) to find out the facts and put that knowledge into practice.

Proper nutrition

As parents, we need to make sure that our student athletes are getting the appropriate nutrition for their age, their sport, and their level of involvement. But nutrition is about more than whether your athlete is getting 'good' or 'bad' food. "Nutrition to enhance athletic performance involves not only what to eat, but when to eat it," said Keith Wheeler, global director of Performance Nutrition, Research and Development at Abbott Nutrition. "When athletes don't consume important nutrients in the right ratios at the right time, they will deplete their bodies and compromise their ability to perform."[1]

While coaches and trainers are good resources, parents need to research on their own as well. There are many resources that will help sports parents understand and prepare for the nutritional needs of their athletes; reputable organizations, sports nutritionists, and sports medicine departments at hospitals and universities can help you and your student apply these principles correctly.

According to Dr. Wheeler: "Nutrition education is critically important for younger athletes who have dual nutrition requirements for their growing bodies and as fuel for training and performance. Yet, high school athletes often are exposed to a range of conflicting health and nutrition messages from a variety of sources. Coaches and parents can help by talking to their kids about safe diet and nutrition practices. Enlisting the help of a registered dietitian experienced with student athletes is a good place to start. A dietitian can provide tailored recommendations that balance the demands of training and busy schedules."[2]

Nutrition is not a "one size fits all" reality. The age and gender of your children, as well as the sport they play, will affect their nutritional needs. So as a parent, you need to know what good nutrition looks like for your student as well as the signs of nutritional traps such as supplements, fads or serious disorders. Making sure your athlete has good nutritional habits will help her play to the best of her ability and will establish a good foundation for the future.

But good nutrition also includes proper hydration. Many parents are surprised to learn that athletes should drink water every 15-20 minutes during activity.[3] They also need to replace important nutrients, such as electrolytes, if their sport requires longer periods of activity (over an hour).[4] Poor fluid intake can lead to heat stroke and dehydration, so parents need to make sure their student is drinking enough of the right things. You cannot rely solely on coaches to implement good hydration policies. Learn the guidelines and teach your child to follow them, regardless of what any other parents or coaches are doing.

Lastly, helping our athletes develop good nutrition means helping them avoid substance abuse. I am aware that a paragraph or two is not sufficient to address the full scope of this topic, but it is important to mention it anyway. Parents must get and stay current on the range of chemicals available to tempt their athletes. At the very least, parents need to be aware of the two primary forms of substance abuse: illegal drugs and performance enhancing supplements.

Many athletes use drugs and alcohol to relieve pressure, to look cool or to mimic the high achieved during competition.[5] But these substances are dangerous traps. We can easily name countless examples of athletes whose careers were destroyed because of an addiction. Even worse, these habits, once in place, are very difficult to break, and the use of these substances often leads to a variety of long-term consequences.

During a neighbor's graduation party one spring, I was lamenting with other sports parents about the arduous process of helping our children make a good college choice. We bemoaned the effort required to interview coaches, professors, and others. As we were talking, another parent spoke up, "While all of you were interviewing schools, I was interviewing lawyers to deal with my son's drug possession charge!" He said it light-heartedly, but I could see the pain below the surface. And unfortunately, his son, a former high school football player, has since had other challenges with substance abuse.

Thankfully, there are many programs designed to warn students about the dangers of these substances. But despite all the warnings, our athletes are tempted to use at younger ages every year. I asked my son when he first encountered students using drugs, and he said, "Mom, kids in middle school are drinking and using drugs." No matter how young your children are, you must talk to them about these substances and do whatever you can to help them avoid these dangerous habits.

However, illegal drugs are not the only temptation our students face. Performance enhancing drugs are another major cause for concern. Supplements that promise bigger, faster results are nothing new, and they are a $3 billion a year business.[6] But they can be very dangerous. They rarely produce the promised results, and they can actually have serious side effects and long-term consequences. Still, many athletes are willing to risk those problems and use these substances anyway.

So what can parents do? Dr. Wheeler's advice is simple and effective. "Sports nutrition products such as EAS protein shakes and bars offer a safe, effective and convenient way for athletes of all levels to get the nutrients they need to maintain an active and busy schedule. Whenever in doubt about a sports product or supplement consult a professional dietitian and do your research."[7]

Clearly, good nutrition is vital for an athlete's success. As a parent, you must do whatever you can to encourage your student to develop good nutritional habits and to avoid the pitfalls of substance abuse throughout his or her athletic career.

On-field safety concerns
The second important safety area that sports parents need to focus on is helping their students reduce the possibility of injury.

126

Sports participation is a major cause of injuries to students every year. According to the National Center for Sports Safety, more than 3.5 million children under the age of 14 receive medical treatment for sports injuries each year.[8] And surprisingly, over 60% of sports-related injuries happen during practice, rather than games.[9] That means that every single time your student steps onto a field he is putting himself at risk of an injury.

Despite that reality, however, most parents do not take an active role in on-field safety issues. According to a Safe Kids report on sports safety, nine out of ten parents rely heavily on coaches to keep their kids safe, and three of four students do the same.[10] While on some levels that reliance makes sense, it is not the best way to keep our children safe.

Not every coach has sufficient training in safety procedures. And for team sports, the coach may have twenty or more students to attend to at all times, making it that much easier for an injury or accident to occur. Coaches cannot be the only defense standing between your child and an injury. Parents must actively participate in the safety policies in place for your student's situation.

So what can a parent do? Active participation can be as simple as getting CPR and first aid training and carrying a first aid kit to every game and practice. Parents can get even more extensive training, but the point is to make sure that someone is always prepared in the case of an emergency. However, whether you get first aid training or not, every parent should be armed with the facts about the most common injuries that occur in the world of student athletics.

The first injury that parents must be aware of is the concussion. Concussions are one of the most common injuries in sports today. In fact, according to Tamerah Hunt, assistant professor at The Ohio State University and director of research at the OSU Sports Concussion program, "Concussion has reached near-epidemic proportions in contact sports at both the professional and amateur levels, with an estimated 1.6 to 3.8 million sports-related concussions occurring in the US every year."[11]

And even though much is said about the danger of concussions, on-field attitudes about them have not changed enough. In the Safe Kids research study, half of the coaches surveyed believed that some amount of head contact is not a problem for young athletes.[12] And many parents and athletes function the same way. These attitudes cannot continue. Concussions are serious injuries, and since 90 percent of concussions happen without the child losing consciousness,[13] every blow to the head must be taken seriously. Parents need to know the warning signs of a concussion, and they must actively encourage their athletes to think and act in ways that reduces their risk for a head injury.[14]

Overuse injuries are the second common problem that parents must be informed about. Overuse injuries involve the athlete's joints, muscles, tendons and ligaments, and include carpal tunnel, tennis elbow, ACL and Achilles tendon strains, and stress fractures. Often these issues are difficult to spot because they develop slowly, but they need to be treated and rehabilitated correctly or they can develop into more significant problems later.[15]

Unfortunately, overuse injuries are tremendously common, and every active person is at risk.[16] But for those competing in athletics on a regular basis, that risk is even higher. A recent study indicated, for example, that soccer players, elite distance runners, wrestlers and weight lifters are at increased risk of ACL strains.[17] Achilles tendon injuries "occur in everything from young kids playing sport to weekend warriors."[18] And teenage girls develop such injuries 6 to 10 times more often than teenage boys because, while both gain height at puberty, girls' muscles do not develop as much as the boys' muscles do.[19] Clearly, this kind of injury warrants a parent's attention.

Thankfully, parents can help their athletes avoid overuse injuries. First, ensure your student gets enough rest. Athletes need to take one or two days off every week, and two to three months off from their sport every year.[20] The strain of athletic competition can be hard on the still-developing bodies of young athletes, so make sure that your student gets the rest he or she needs to stay at full health.

This rest is even more important when an athlete is recovering from an injury. Unfortunately, though, many coaches have felt pressured by parents and athletes to play an injured child,[21] and three out of ten students (44% of boys aged 15-18) believe that an athlete should play with an injury until someone makes them stop.[22] We must not condone such attitudes. As an advocate for your child, make sure that no one, not your child, the coach or even you, is pushing the child to compete until an injury has been properly and completely rehabilitated.

Second, parents need to guard against an over-emphasis on a particular joint or movement. Repetitive training drills and sports specialization have resulted in more and more overuse injuries every year.[23] Student athletes who focus on a single sport, especially at a young age, can do serious damage to their bodies. Parents should encourage young children, in particular, to play multiple sports or take time off between seasons so that no one area of their body is under stress for an extended period of time.

Finally, parents need to emphasize, and insist that coaches emphasize, the importance of warming up and stretching. Recent studies have shown that strains to the ACL and Achilles tendon, for example, can be reduced simply by warming up correctly and doing exercises that strengthen the muscles that support those joints. According to Dr. Timothy Hewitt, Director of Sports Medicine at The Ohio State University, training the muscles around the knee joint can decrease the risk of injury to the ACL by up to 60 percent.[24]

Parents need to be attentive to the on-field activity of their athletes to help prevent injuries when possible. Having said this, however, we also need to be careful not to overstep boundaries. As I learned from my broken ankle, parents should not be on the sidelines unnecessarily. And we should not assume the coach is not concerned about safety. Instead, our goal should be to assist the coach, actively assessing the activity on the field so that dangerous play can be stopped before someone gets hurt.

Emotional Safety

Physical safety is an obvious area of concern for sports parents. However, parents who are more than zealous about preventing injury often neglect a less obvious, but equally important area—emotional safety.

According to Dr. Lief Smith, sports and clinical psychologist for the Ohio State Buckeyes and author of *Sports Psychology for Dummies*, "Participating in sports is an emotional experience—sometimes it's intense and painful, and other times it's positive and exciting."[25] No athlete can compete with any passion if she does not engage her emotions. But that emotional investment opens our athletes up to emotional crises as well.

Thousands of students struggle emotionally as they try to balance sports with school, home and a social life. The tensions of winning, of performing to ever higher standards, of earning a scholarship, add stress to the already hectic life of a full-time student. They long to find the balance we discussed in Chapter 4, but many athletes can feel overwhelmed by the requirements for athletic success. Add to those pressures the hormonal changes that the teenage years bring, and we should not be surprised that our students' emotional safety is at risk.

So what can we, as sports parents and advocates, do? How can we help our students manage and avoid the emotional pitfalls the world of athletics can throw in their paths?

The most effective tactic is to be attentive. As we discussed in Chapter 6, we need to listen and support our students. We need to be aware of what is going on in their lives so that we can recognize the warning signs of emotional instability when and if they appear. And we need to focus our attention in three key areas.

Watch for Signs of Burnout

One of the most common emotional issues that athletes face is burnout. As we mentioned in Chapter 7, everyone wants to quit at some point in their lives. And we need to encourage our students to finish their commitments instead of just walking away.

However, it is just as important to be in tune with our athletes so that we recognize their emotional state in this area. And sadly, many parents miss the signals that their athlete is sending out, the subtle signs that he needs a break, that she wants a breather.

According to Dr. Smith, burnout has some very specific indicators. For most students, burnout will show up as a loss of interest in practice, a lack of preparation, a reluctance to do the extras (practicing or working out on their own), various symptoms of depression, a drop in athletic performance, actually stating a desire to stop playing, or talking less about their sport than they used to.[26]

Parents must be on the lookout for any or all of these indicators. We need to take them seriously and talk with our athletes about where they are and whether they need a break. Of course, that is sometimes hard for the committed sports parent to do. As I mentioned in Chapter 7, I struggled with Joshua Odis's decision to leave football, but in the end, it was clear that was the right path for him to follow. When burnout occurs, parents need to be willing to let their athletes get the rest they need, even if it means leaving the sport for good.

And as parents, we must remember not to put too much pressure on our athletes. Often, our quest to help our children achieve their dreams means we do too much for them, and they may come to see our obsession as pressure. While most parents are not intentionally pushing their agenda onto their athlete, most children want to please their parents, so they continue to compete, even if they no longer want to do so. And the result is burnout—when what begins as something fun and rewarding slowly turns into a burden.

As Dr. Smith contends, "Burnout has numerous possible causes but a large one is parents pushing their own desires and dreams on their kids. If your kids remain in sports more for you than for herself, she's never going to reach her highest potential—and she probably won't stay involved in sports as long as she would have otherwise.[27]

We must protect our children's love of their sport, and we must focus as much on whether or not they are enjoying their activity as we do on how they are performing. We must watch for signs of burnout and make sure they get occasional breaks from the constant tension of their sports.

Watch for Signs of Distress

Secondly, for many students, burnout is less a factor than a sense of distress. They do not really want to leave their sport, but they start to flounder under the overwhelming pressure of their daily lives. In the face of the never-ending list of tasks competing for their attention, these children begin to feel as if they will never be able keep up.

It is possible that this kind of emotional frustration may not affect their athletic performance in any way. But it will still manifest itself as irritability, a constant focus on the "next thing" that must be done, physical exhaustion, or a need to get away for a time. As parents, we must be tuned in to these responses in our children, and we need to actively support them as they work through their particular circumstances.

When one of my boys would come home with "that look" on his face, I would start by asking, "Is everything okay?" Sometimes he would tell me right away what was bothering him, but other times, he would brush me off. And even though he would tell me, "It's all right," my gut told me differently. On those days, I would follow my son up the stairs and tell him I really needed to know what was going on. If that didn't work, I would announce that I was setting up camp in his room until he was ready to talk. That usually got the conversation started.

Of course, our students will never confide in us if they do not know that their home is a safe place, physically and emotionally. My boys could be open with me because they knew that nothing they told me would make me stop loving them or supporting them. I also worked hard to listen well and avoid reacting to the first shocking thing that they shared. And I let them know that they could count on me to work with them and deal with whatever situations they were facing.

That kind of partnership is vital to helping our students deal with the emotional distress that is, quite frankly, a part of life.

As we help them work through these stresses, we can model good emotional responses and provide a foundation for how they, too, can learn to adapt and move forward, in sports and in life. As Dr. Smith indicates, "Research has shown and continues to show that parents' behaviors and attitudes have clear influences on their young athletes' motivation levels and psychological development. The feedback and behaviors you demonstrate can influence how long your kid plays sports, how he defines success (for example, winning versus improving), his perception of his own abilities, and his anxiety about sports participation.[28]

Watch for Signs of Abuse
Lastly, but perhaps most importantly, parents must be vigilant about any signs that their athletes are experiencing the emotional devastation of abuse.

Whenever your child is attacked or harmed, they are experiencing abuse. Bullying occurs when the attacker is a peer. When the attacker is a person in power (a coach, trainer, administrator, or other adult), the only appropriate term is abuse. Abuse can be physical, emotional, mental or sexual, and each type is tragic, often leaving long-term scars in the life of the victim.

In the arena of sports, emotional abuse might include name-calling, yelling, threatening, insulting or intimidating a player. Physical abuse would include hitting, kicking, hair-pulling, shoving around, or other bodily assault. And of course, sexual abuse is the inappropriate touching or handling of a child's body.[29]

However, knowing the facts about abuse doesn't always make it easy to detect. The news is flooded with stories of children being bullied at school; coaches and teachers have been arrested for sexually molesting children in their care, and in many cases, the child either believes it is her fault or is too ashamed to report the abuse.

As a sports parent, you can increase your chances of preventing abuse simply by paying attention. Be attentive at games and practices. How does the coach speak to the athletes? How are the other parents interacting with their own (or other) athletes? Being aware of the dynamics surrounding your child's team or sport is the first step towards avoiding abusive situations.

Secondly, listen to your child. What are the athletes talking about? Be nosy. Know the gossip and the chatter. Don't be afraid to check Facebook pages, text messages or emails if you are concerned there may be a problem. And most importantly, pay attention to your child's behavior. Many of the warning signs of abuse are similar to the warning signs of distress and burnout. Abused athletes might try to avoid practices or riding the bus. They might show signs of depression or suddenly stop talking to you altogether. Know what is normal for your child and then watch for behaviors that suddenly seem unusual or out of place in your student's life.

Whatever else you do, never leave your child in an unhealthy situation. Investigate thoroughly any concerns you have so that you do not accuse an innocent person. But walking away from abusive coaches and dangerous situations is not only necessary, it is wise. We all know far too many stories of abused and bullied children and the consequences of those experiences. Be tuned in to your child, watch for warning signs, give credence to his fears, and do whatever it takes to protect your child from harmful situations.

Conclusion
Sports participation offers our students tremendous benefits academically, socially, and physically. But athletics also opens the doors to certain risks that sports parents must address.

No matter how much you believe in a coach or a program, never let your loyalty to a program, school system, community or person override your good sense and responsibility as a parent. One of our highest priorities as sports parents must be to keep our children, and their teammates, safe.

We cannot rely solely on a coach or a program to guard our athletes' health and well-being. We must be involved as well. We should not worry needlessly, inventing problems where none actually exist. But we do need to be vigilant and alert to the signs of physical and emotional trauma in our athletes.

Our children's safety is paramount!

Endnotes

[1]Keith Wheeler, email to author, 27 Sept. 2012.

[2]Wheeler, email to author, 27 Sept. 2012.

[3]*Sports Safety Tip Sheet for Parents and Coaches*, 2012, Safe Kids Worldwide, 25 Sept. 2012 <www.safekids.org>

[4]"Sports Drinks," OSU Sports Medicine, 26 Sept. 2012 <http://sportsmedicine.osu.edu/patientcare/sports_nutrit ion/drinks>

[5]Linda Ray, "The Effects of Drugs and Alcohol on Youth Athletes," 12 May 2011, Livestrong. 1 Oct. 2012 <http://www.livestrong.com/article/437298-the-effects-of-drugs-alcohol-on-youth-athletes/>

[6]"Performance Enhancers," OSU Sports Medicine, 1 Oct. 2012 <http://sportsmedicine.osu.edu/patientcare/sports_nutrition/ performanceenhancers/>

[7]Wheeler, email to author, 27 Sept. 2012.

[8]"Sports Injury Facts," 2012, National Center for Sports Safety. 25 Sept 2012 <http://www.sportssafety.org/sports-injury-facts>

[9]*Sports and Recreation Safety in the USA*, 2012, Safe Kids Worldwide. 25 Sept 2012 <www.safekids.org.>

[10]*Coaching our Kids to Fewer Injuries: A Report on Youth Sports Safety*, 2012, Safe Kids Worldwide, 25 Sept. 2012: 2

[11]Diane Kukich, "Concussion Expert Visits Campus," 26 Oct. 2011, UDaily. 4 Oct. 2012 <http://www.udel.edu/udaily/2012/oct/hunt-concussions-102611.html>

[12]*Coaching our Kids* 3.

[13]*Coaching our Kids* 18.

[14]*Concussion Fact Sheet for Parents*, 2012, Safe Kids Worldwide, 25 Sept 2012 <www.safekids.org.>

[15]Lyle Micheli, *Overuse Injuries: The New Scourge of Kids Sports*, 2012, National Center for Sports Safety. 4 Oct. 2012   <www.sportssafety.org/articles/kids-overuse-injuries/>

[16]Joseph Iero, *Chronic or Overuse Injuries in Sports*, 2012, National Center for Sports Safety. 25 Sept. 2012 <www.sportssafety.org/articles/chronic-overuse-injuries/>

[17]Cindy Kuzma, "Save Your Knees—Now," 11 Nov. 2011,   Men's   Health.   4   Oct.   2012 <http://news.menshealth.com/knee-pain-and-osteoarthritis-prevention/2011/11/11/>

[18]"Simple Steps to Avoid Painful Achilles Injury," 28 March   2012,   ABC2news.   4   Oct.   2012 <http://www.abc2news.com/dpp/news/health/simple-steps-to-avoid-painful-achilles-injury>

[19]Genevra Pittman, "Warm-ups Cut Sports Injuries in Teen Girls: Study," 10 Nov. 2011, Reuters Health. 4 Oct. 2012   <http://www.reuters.com/article/2011/11/11/us-warm-ups-cut-teen-idUSTRE7AA03L20111111>

[20]*Coaching our Kids* 10.

[21]*Coaching our Kids* 3.

[22]*Coaching our Kids* 17.

[23]Micheli,   <www.sportssafety.org/articles/kids-overuse-injuries/>

[24]Kuzma, <http://news.menshealth.com/knee-pain-and-osteoarthritis-prevention/2011/11/11/>

[25]Lief Smith, *Sports Psychology for Dummies* (Mississauga, ON: Wiley, 2010) 266.

[26]Smith 275.

[27]Smith 264.

[28]Smith 279.

[29]Brooke de Lench, "Abuse in Youth Sports Takes Many Different Forms," 29 Sept. 2011, momsTEAM.com. 3   Oct.   2012.   <http://www.momsteam.com/health-

safety/emotional-injuries/general/abuse-in-youth-sports-takes-many-different-forms>

Chapter Eight
Pursuing Persistence (Never Give Up!)

And let us not grow weary of doing good, for in due season
we will reap, if we do not give up. Galatians 6:9

"If at first you don't succeed..."
Learning to drive a car is always a memorable experience. Especially when it's your son or daughter getting behind the wheel.

Jay learned to drive during a particularly snowy winter, and our Lincoln Continental had a really long front end as well as brakes and power steering that required a lighter touch than Jay was used to delivering. We endured months of zigzag driving and being slammed around in our seats as he steered and applied the brakes. It was not pleasant. Thankfully, he did get better, and now he is a careful and attentive driver—at least while he's driving my car!

Driving always looks easy from the backseat. But once behind the wheel, we quickly discover that driving well is not easy at all. It is hard at first to check all the mirrors at once, to know how much pressure to use on the brake, to park in the center of a parking space (and some people never do learn this one). Learning to drive takes time and practice and lots and lots of mistakes.

Just like sports. Just like life.

No matter what we or our athletes hope to achieve, it will take time and energy. It will mean setbacks and failures. None of us will reach our dream with one giant step. That's why the most important quality we need to develop, and help our students to develop, is persistence.

Persistence means a total commitment to pursuing your dreams. It means trying until you get it right. It's choosing to keep fighting, even when you feel like giving up; it's refusing to let failures and mistakes keep you from your goals. And it is the only way to succeed, in sports and in life.

Keep On Keepin' On
In sports, persistence is vital.

Basic skills such as dribbling, passing, throwing, catching, and swinging a bat or club must be practiced innumerable times. Each element of a tumbling pass must be perfected on its own before it can be combined with others. Athletes spend hours in the water, in the gym, on the field, going over and over their skills until they can do them perfectly, every time.

And mental persistence is just as important. An athlete has to think like a football player, a soccer player, a golfer.

141

He has to learn which plays to run, which offensive or defensive patterns to call, which strategies to use during a particular game. She has to learn to make decisions at a moment's notice, even under pressure. And that kind of mental sharpness does not come overnight. It is developed, practiced, learned...only by persistence.

We must teach our students to be persistent in these ways. But physical and mental persistence will not be sufficient to ensure their success. We must do more than simply encourage our athletes to keep training, keep learning, and keep working hard so that they can achieve their dreams. We must help our students to develop a third kind of persistence.

In order to reach their dreams, our athletes will need *emotional* persistence most of all.

Emotional persistence is the maturity to choose to keep going, no matter what; To practice your free throw again. To run the play one more time; To work hard all day on a particular goal and then go out tomorrow and do it all again.

Emotional persistence means that no matter how rough it gets, no matter how inconvenient, no matter how much we feel like walking away, we stick it out. We keep going. We refuse to allow how we feel to determine how we act. We are all-in—until our commitment is fulfilled or our goal is reached.

In other words, we decide that, whether in sports or in life, quitting is not an option.

Emotional persistence is necessary to success, on and off the field. A person who can finish her commitments, who can keep going during the rough times, will be able to succeed no matter her goal. And as parents, it is our job to teach our students to function that way, to help them develop that kind of tenacity, to make sure they understand that quitting should always be the very last option.

Parenting Persistence

Of course, that sounds great. Obviously, no parent wants her children to throw in the towel in the tough moments or to quit at the least sign of trouble. But how do we do this? How do we help our children develop emotional persistence?

Start by establishing the expectation for your children. As soon as you can, set the standard that they will not be permitted to quit, to walk away from a commitment, without a serious and valid reason.

I tried hard to teach my boys this principle. Before they ever signed up to play a sport, I made it clear that they would be expected to stick it out until the end. It was important to me that they learn to follow through on their commitments.

Then one Saturday morning during little league football, Joshua Alexander decided that it was too early and too cold to go to practice. So he announced that he was staying home. I, however, had different plans. I reminded Josh of his commitment and insisted that he get dressed and get going. He didn't like it, but he went. And of course, once he got there, he was fine.

For Joshua, the standard had been set. Long before that cold morning, I had discussed with him what he would need to do to play football. There was no changing my mind, and he knew the rule, so he knew he had no choice but to get dressed and out the door.

And that is the first step: if we want our children to develop emotional persistence, we have to expect them to be persistent.

The truth is, most children are willing and able to rise to the expectations that are set for them. If we coddle them, they will learn that they can do very little and get by. If we expect them to quit, they will. But if we set the standard high, they will learn that, with a little effort, they can do more than they realized they could. If we expect them to keep trying, they will learn to be persistent; they will discover that they can keep going and accomplish great things.

Opting In or Opting Out?

So the first part of helping our students develop emotional persistence is to establish that expectation and hold them to it. On that Saturday morning, Joshua Alexander learned that I was serious when I said that my sons would follow through on their commitments.

But he also experienced the second part of emotional persistence: the moment of choice.

Finishing our commitments is really about making choices. Every day, over and over, we have to choose whether to keep going or to walk away. And the choice we make will always be based either on how we *think* or on how we *feel*.

Our students will never develop persistence if they base their decisions on their feelings. On that Saturday morning, Joshua had decided that the cold weather and the early hour were good enough reasons not to go to practice. But those were just excuses. The real issue wasn't the weather or the time; it was that Joshua didn't *feel like* going to practice.

And to be fair, the feeling itself is not the problem; it's part of being human. At some point, we all *feel like* quitting. At some point, we don't want to go to school or to the gym. We won't care about doing homework or practicing free throws before bed. Eventually, every road gets rough. And your child is no different. She will face a difficult season, an injury, a major setback to her dream, and she will feel like walking away.

That is the moment of choice. To stay or to go. To stick it out or to throw in the towel. And that is the moment where we, as parents, have a real opportunity to help our children choose well.

In those moments, we must acknowledge how they feel and walk them through the decision. They may need us to encourage them to try one more time, even though they are frustrated and want to walk away. We might have to navigate them through weeks of intense discussions. But we must teach them how to choose well because thoughtful choices are the only foundation on which persistence can be truly formed.

By talking our children through how they feel and encouraging them to stay on track anyway, they learn to choose maturely and with endurance. As we walk them through their options, we can help them realize that a commitment to a sport, a team, or an athletic dream is more important than how they *feel*. And gradually, they will learn to make thoughtful choices consistently: to keep going, despite how they're feeling, until they have reached their goals.

To Quit or Not To Quit?

Of course, in athletics, these moments of choice are normal. Almost every athlete has to decide, at some point, whether to quit her sport or to push on to the next level.

He may have competed in his sport for years, spending countless hours practicing, living away from family, sacrificing time with friends and a "normal" life for the sake of his dream. And then, one morning, he wonders whether he really wants to keep going, whether all the work and time are worth the cost, whether his dream is really still alive.

If you are a sports parent, your athlete will face that moment. It is going to happen. So what should you do? How can you best help them work through that difficult and important decision?

Start by talking to them.

There are probably many factors influencing your student's desire to quit, so get inside her head and find out what is going on. This will require the listening and paying attention we talked about in Chapter 6. But it also requires another powerful tool—discernment.

Discernment is the ability to judge well. It means that you see what is really going on, even if it's not immediately obvious. It means hearing what is being said as well as what is NOT being said, what is being left out. It is being clued in to our children, gaining insight into their feelings and motives so you can help them make their decision.

Being a discerning parent is particularly important when the issue is persistence because *not all quitting is the same*. Sometimes it is hard to tell whether a request to quit is because your athlete is giving up or because of some deeper issue. And as a parent and an advocate, you have to know the difference.

Fighting Fear

In some cases, your child may say he wants to quit when he really means that he is afraid. And fear is a powerful motivator, especially in a child.

As parents, we must take our child's fears seriously because, sometimes, fear is a cautionary sign. Gaven De Becker describes fear as "a brilliant internal guardian that stands ready to warn you of hazards and guide you through risky situations."[1] In other words, fear can be a red flag. So you need to know the difference between a lack of persistence and a sincere cry for help in your particular child.

When it comes to fear, you cannot be too careful. These days, there are too many instances of abuse and bullying to ignore even the slightest warning signs. If you have any concerns at all about your child's situation, trust your instincts. If you think something is not right, stop by practice and observe the dynamic between your child and his coaches and teammates. Take your child's fears seriously and do whatever it takes to protect him from harmful situations. When your child is in danger, walking away is not quitting...it is wise.

Thankfully, that kind of circumstance is rare. Most children do not have to fear a person or a dangerous situation. Instead, he might be afraid of failing. He might be afraid of injury. Of not being as good as someone else. He might fear criticism—from a coach, a teammate, or even you.

And these fears are just as powerful. As parents, we must take these fears seriously as well.

I once read that FEAR is really **F**alse **E**xpectations **A**ppearing **R**eal. And so often, that is the case. The things that our children fear are probably not going to happen. But they don't realize that. They see only what they fear, and they shrink from it. They do not want to face it; they want to walk away.

That is where you must step in. If you discover fear is motivating her desire to quit, encourage her to stick it out. Talk about fear itself. Share stories of your own failures and the results. Help her to see past the fear to the possibilities and encourage her to finish her commitment.

Afraid of Heights?

On the other hand, it is also possible that your student is afraid, not of failure, but of success. Consider this quote by Marianne Williamson: "Our deepest fear is not that we are inadequate. Our deepest fear is that we are powerful beyond measure. It is our light, not our darkness that most frightens us. We ask ourselves, who am I to be brilliant, gorgeous, talented and fabulous?"

We must realize that some of our children know that, if they work hard, they can accomplish well more than their classmates, their teammates, their friends. And they are afraid. Afraid to achieve more than the average. Afraid that they will reach the pinnacle of their sport or activity and...then what? They will have nowhere to go but down. So they fear what comes after.

How do you help a child who is afraid of her "light"? First of all, assure her that your love or approval of her does not and will not depend on her success or failure. Her abilities are not what make her valuable to you. You want her to push higher, but your love will never be affected by the heights (or depths) that result from her attempts. The greater value is to keep trying.

But we can also encourage our students to embrace their gifts. Ms. Williamson continues: "Actually, who are we not to be [brilliant, gorgeous, talented and fabulous]? You are a child of God. Your playing small does not serve the world...We are all meant to shine as children do. We are born to manifest the glory of God that is within us. It's not just in some of us; it's in everyone."[2]

Remind your children that God has given each of us special talents. The ability to succeed in a sport is a gift, a precious grace, and they should humbly receive it. They do not have to fear the failures or successes they experience on the way to achieving their dreams, but instead should live the best life they can. Encourage them to keep their commitments, trusting that the God who gifted them so richly can also manage the outcome.

On to Plan B?
So, sometimes what looks like quitting is really fear. But other times, quitting is...just quitting. They really do want to stop. They want out. They are done playing, and they have no desire or intention to continue on this path.

When it becomes clear that this is the case, what should you do?

Again, discernment is the key. Talk to your child. Discuss, in detail, why your student wants to quit, and talk with her about why it is so important to stick with a commitment she has made. Make sure he understands the magnitude of his decision. We need to ensure that our students think the decision all the way through.

One of the best ways to do this is to have them consider the consequences of quitting. Ask them to write down the possible repercussions that leaving in the middle of their commitment might have. Are they really prepared to deal with the fallout of quitting?

For example, quitting can cost them their reputation. Do they want to be seen as immature or irresponsible? Are they prepared to deal with coaches or officials who will consider them selfish or unreliable? This is often how others respond to those who quit without completing their commitments, so the potential damage to their reputation needs to be considered.

Quitting will also affect their team. Who will fill in the position that they played? Without them there, the rest of the team will have to scramble to plug the hole that is left. But the roster is not all that will be affected. The team dynamic will also be impacted. As a team works together during games and practices, teammates learn to read each other, to know each player's strengths and weaknesses. When someone quits unexpectedly, that dynamic is immediately upset. Are they really okay with deserting their team that way?

Most importantly, they need to consider the long-term consequences. Quitting can be a slippery slope. The more they do it, the easier it gets. And if they aren't careful, quitting can become a bad habit, a habit that can lead to much bigger problems.

I have personally observed what can happen when a child is allowed to quit without a truly good reason to do so. As quitting becomes a habit, the student can begin to feel left out and withdraws. This distance then makes him vulnerable to even more devastating influences like running with the wrong crowd or turning to drugs or alcohol, creating even more distance than before. It becomes a vicious cycle.

Obviously, no one intends to become a habitual quitter. In fact, most habitual quitters don't see themselves that way. They have lots of "good" reasons for not completing their commitments: they don't like the coach, they're struggling to learn a skill, they got passed over for the starting position, they just want more time to themselves. But those are just excuses. The real issue is the expectation that everything should come easily. They don't want to have to work hard. So when circumstances get difficult, they give up.

Quitting "just because" cannot be allowed. We must teach our children that life is not easy, nor should they expect it to be. As parents, we must ask our students to honestly assess *why* they want to quit. Do they have a legitimate reason, or do they want an "easy-out"? They need to understand their own motivations so they can avoid the slippery slope of habitual quitting.

We need to help them see difficult situations, not as personal insults, but as learning opportunities, as chances to learn how to deal with difficult people or how to "play second fiddle" well. Show them that persistence is the best way to prepare themselves for the rest of their lives.

But, even after all that, they may still want to quit.

It may be that your student really does long to follow a different path, that she has a new dream she wants to pursue. And in that case, it is not, strictly speaking, quitting. Instead, it is redirection. As long as he has fulfilled his obligations to his first commitment (by finishing out the season, for example), you can let him follow his new path without concern, continuing to act as his advocate in his new venture.

Of course, that sounds much easier than it is, as I learned from experience.

When Joshua Odis, our youngest, decided to play football, I was concerned. He had never liked athletic activities and especially didn't like being hit. I told him I didn't think it was a good idea, that he didn't have to play football just because his brothers did. I felt that he was under a lot of pressure from other people, but he insisted that he wanted to try it out and that he was genuinely interested in learning to play.

He played for two seasons, and sometimes I could tell he was not having a lot of fun. To his credit, he kept at it and learned the dynamics. However, although he honored his commitment, I could tell he would rather be doing something else.

Then, before his freshman year in high school, he announced that he was done playing football and nothing would change his mind. I gently reminded him that I was the one who thought he should not play at all. He said he had genuinely wanted to play at the time, but he had learned that football wasn't for him. He was firm about his decision and focused on track instead.

Did Joshua Odis quit? Yes and no. He stopped playing football. So in that sense, he did quit the game. But how he did so proved that he is not a quitter. He finished all his obligations, making sure he left no one depending on him. He discussed the issues, made his decision, and then committed himself to a new path which he pursued with the same level of consistency and dedication.

While it is always important that they finish out their commitments, our children need the freedom to discover who they are and where they want to go and to pursue that wholeheartedly, even if it means redirecting their steps into new avenues along the way. The choice to walk away from one path does not necessarily mean your student lacks persistence. You must look at the bigger picture. If they are firmly committed to the new path, let them make the switch. They will persistently pursue their dreams until they succeed.

Persistent Parenting

Persistence is a powerful tool that will help our athletes achieve their dreams. But our students are not the only ones who need to develop persistence. As sports parents, we, too, must develop a habit of living with persistence, particularly as we parent our children.

We need to model for our students the principles of persistence that we want them to develop. In your own life, refuse to give up in the difficult times. Keep your commitments, no matter the cost. Show them what it means to work through failures and setbacks until you finally reach your goal.

Above all, persistent parenting means never giving up on our children. It means supporting our athletes, encouraging them to be the best that they can be, always believing in them, and communicating that support at every opportunity. It means truly being their advocate, always.

On the other hand, however, we need to have a balanced persistence. Sports parents must be careful that we stay focused on our child, not just her athletic dream.

For many parents, it's all too easy to get so caught up in the daily demands of advocating for our athlete that we begin to focus more on the dream than on the child who dreams it. And that must never happen. We must maintain a balance between the details of schedules, scholarship applications, and steps towards success and the reality of what is actually best for our children. We cannot focus on his or her career more than we do on our child as a person.

And this is especially true when they are considering leaving their particular sport.

When Joshua Odis announced that he no longer wanted to play football, I struggled with this dilemma. After two years of seeing him play, I had started to dream of having my third child on the high school team and to think about how much fun it would be to have four more years of this experience. His desire to quit football forced me to stop and reevaluate my own focus.

Did I want the life of a football mom more than I wanted what was best for Joshua Odis? It was a difficult question, but so very important. I had to wake up and realize that my dream for him was not in his best interest. He still needed me to be persistent, but not in the pursuit of football. He needed me to be persistent in parenting him.

Knowing what is best for our student takes discernment. Sometimes, she will need a little nudge, some small encouragement to keep going, and she will find her groove again. Other times, he will need you to let him pursue a new path. That was true for Joshua Odis. Pushing him to stay with football would have led only to resentment. Talking with him made it very clear that his decision was made, and I had to trust that his reasoning was good (and it was).

Persistent parenting means focusing on the person you want your child to become, not keeping her in a sport she no longer loves. You may not want him to quit playing, but if, after calm and thoughtful discussions, he still wants to walk away, then it's time to step aside. Just because she is doing well doesn't mean she's having a good time. Great stats, scholarship offers, and championship trophies mean nothing if he longs to do something else. Listen carefully so you'll be able to discern when he has truly had enough. Your job is to ask the tough questions, help her think through the issues, refuse to pressure her, and then support her final call—persistently.

Long-Term Success

Clearly, persistence is important. It is one of the most valuable disciplines that we and our students can develop. But life is not a sprint. The pursuit of a dream is a long and winding road. Raising our children well is a marathon event. In sports and in life, we have to be committed for the long haul.

To be truly persistent, we must never lose that long-term perspective.

There will be times when we will have to remind our students to keep going. No athlete always wants to practice. No student always wants to study that one last chapter. So we will have to encourage our student athletes to keep focused on the big goal and keep taking the little steps that will get them there.

And as parents, there will be times when we have to remind ourselves to keep going, too. No child always listens to her mother. Eventually, every child is going to ignore his daddy's advice. As my mother often said, "We sometimes talk until we are blue in the face," and still we don't see much evidence that our training is making a difference.

But I promise you—persistence will always pay off in the end. Consider the Chinese bamboo tree.

It requires great patience to grow Chinese bamboo. You pick the spot, prepare the soil, and then plant the tree. You water it and wait. But after an entire year, nothing appears. No bud, no twig, nothing. So you keep watering the ground and wait some more. At the end of the second year, still nothing. You water some more, check the soil. You start talking to the ground, maybe even prance around in some kind of growing dance you saw on National Geographic. Three years pass—and still no sign of growth.

Should you give up? Probably. But someone told you that it might take a while to really see the fruits of your efforts, so you keep on keeping on. More water, more talk, more dancing. The neighbors are starting to talk. Especially when year four passes and still no bamboo.

But you are undeterred. You set out to grow a bamboo tree, and you don't intend to give up now. You begin year number five with the same passion as day number one. You water, you wait. You keep watering and keep waiting. You water some more and then...wait! Could it be? Is it really?

Yes, there is something right there, a small green *something* sticking out of the dirt. All your hard work is finally paying off. And paying off in a big way. Because when you come back the next day, WOW! It has really grown! In fact, the Chinese Bamboo will grow 1-2 inches every day for six weeks, and when it stops growing, it will be over 80 feet tall! That's right, 80 feet in six weeks!

Well, not really. It grows 80 feet in five years. But the growth is only visible for those final six weeks.

The point is obvious. If you had given up for even the shortest period of time, there would be no tree. It took almost impossible persistence. The Chinese Bamboo tree is there for one reason and one reason only—because you never gave up on it.

Your child is just like that Chinese Bamboo tree. Your child's dream is like that tree, too. You both will have to keep watering and cultivating even when you don't see much growth. You'll have to remind yourselves that there is a lot happening under the surface that can't always be seen with the natural eye, but it is still happening.

As parents and advocates, we must pursue that growth in our athletes, even when we can't see any evidence of it at all. We have to keep picking them up and dusting them off even when they feel they can't go on.

And we must train our athlete to do the same. Teach him to be persistent, to keep going even when the going is tough and the goal seems impossible to reach. Teach her to continue doing the little things every day that will lead, over time, to major achievements, college scholarships, and the accomplishment of her deepest dreams. Remind him that the race doesn't always go to the swift, but to the person who endures to the end.

Be persistent in parenting your children. Be consistent in teaching them to be persistent, too. And some day (in the not-so-distant future), you will look up, and your child will have grown into the most amazing person. More than just a wonderful athlete, you will have helped to create a solid citizen, a dedicated student, a hard worker, a committed friend.

Never give up on your child, and in the end, they will learn not to give up on all they were born to be.

End Notes
[1] "The Gift of Fear Quotes," GoodReads, 2012. 12 Nov. 2012 <http://www.goodreads.com/work/quotes/1212277-gift-of-fear-survival-signals-that-protect-us-from-violence>.
[2] Williamson, Marianne, *A Return to Love.* 12 Nov. 2012. <www.marianne.com>

About the Author

Deborah Johnson, AKA "DJ the Sports Mom" is an accomplished educator, inspirational speaker, writer and storyteller. She is the president of Goal Minded, LLC, which is an organization that advocates for and teaches sports parents how to prepare their children for success in life through sports. Deborah was the "NFL SpokesMom" for the Campbell Soup Company's 2011 "Address Your Heart" campaign. Deborah won the Dr. Oz NFL Mom Ultimate Health Challenge in 2010. She is the co-founder of the Football Parents Association at Ohio State, Member of the Professional Football Players Mothers Association and she sits on the National Alliance for Youth Sports Board. She is also the co-host of Game Ready Mom radio Deborah earned a B.A. in French from The Ohio State University and a Masters in Human Services Management from Brandeis University.

Two of her sons earned D-1 college football scholarships and all of her sons played varsity sports. She is a passionate sports parent advocate. She and her husband, Glen, reside in Powell, Ohio.

For information on booking DJ as a speaker, contact her via email at footballmom99@sbcglobal.net or by phone at 614-733-8910.

Made in the USA
Lexington, KY
23 April 2014